4/2.8 5M

SICILY

Recipes from an Italian island

OTHER BOOKS BY KATIE & GIANCARLO CALDESI

The Amalfi Coast: A Collection of Italian Recipes
Venice: Recipes Lost and Found
Rome: Centuries in an Italian Kitchen

RECIPE NOTES

— Unless otherwise stated: all fruit and vegetables are
  medium-sized; all fruit and herbs are fresh; all eggs are
  free-range and medium-sized.

— All olive oil used in this book is extra-virgin olive oil.

— Raw or lightly cooked eggs should be avoided by pregnant
  women, the elderly and very young children.

— Recipes that contain nuts should be avoided by those
  with a known allergic reaction to nuts and nut derivatives.

— Oven temperature: these are given for fan ovens. If you are
  using a conventional oven, increase the heat by around
  20°C (you can also check with the manufacturer's
  handbook).

To Teresa

SICILY

Recipes from an Italian island

BY KATIE & GIANCARLO CALDESI

Viva Sicilia!
Enjoy te recipes from
this crazy + brilliant
island!

Katie Caldesi

ILLUSTRATIONS BY JOHANNA NOACK
PHOTOGRAPHY BY HELEN CATHCART

hardie grant books

CONTENTS

INTRODUCTION

Sicily is a unique and extraordinary tapestry – intricate, vibrant and brightly coloured in parts, shot through with exquisite strands of gold and silver; worn bare, faded and patched up in others. Look behind the fabric holding it together and you will see a complex tangle of thousands of threads that give it its outward appearance. Like all treasured possessions, it has passed through the hands of various owners, each leaving their mark.

From the 7th century BC, the Phoenicians, Greeks, Romans and Arabs invaded Sicily, followed by the Normans, Spanish and more. When I started researching Sicilian food, I thought I could unpick these threads and follow them back to their source to see singular origins for particular dishes. I would be able to say with assurance, 'This is an Arabic recipe from the west of the island, this is Greek from the east,' and so on, but it is not as simple as that. Actually, the tapestry is very tightly woven; it is impossible to unravel. Sicily's culture as well as its cuisine is the result of all of these threads knotted together. It is this exotic mixture of influences from the East and West that makes the Sicilian kitchen so different from the rest of Italy.

The *cassata*, a sweet ricotta-filled sponge cake covered in green icing (frosting) and decorated with jewels of candied fruit, is a perfect example of this; it is the history of a cake and an island. The name comes possibly from the Arabs, who used a domed dish called a *qas'at*, or from the Latin for cheese, *caseum*. The Greeks made ricotta-style cheese but the Arabs brought over sugar cane and sweetened it and flavoured it with citrus fruits, almonds and cinnamon. During the Norman period, marzipan came into vogue and the *cassata's* pastry case was cast off in favour of the new almond paste. The Spanish introduced a light layer of sponge and added bitter chocolate to contrast with the sweet ricotta. The English coated the cake in icing, which made it last longer, and finally during the baroque period of the 18th century, bright candied fruit and intricate swirls of icing were added to top the whole creation.

Sicily is the largest island in the Mediterranean and is the market of Italy. Nowhere else can boast the variety and quality of its natural produce, the best and freshest fish from clear blue waters, fruits of every kind ripened in the hot sun, sheep and goat cheeses from the mountains.

As Giancarlo and I drove up the winding road to Polizzi Generosa, towards central Sicily, we passed jujube trees, fig, walnut, apple and pear trees laden with their autumn harvest. With fish from the sea, game from the land and the ability to grow crops easily on the fertile soil, it is easy to see why people would want to settle there. It is a natural paradise yet over the years it has been ravaged not only by some of the cruellest invaders from the outside but also by the Mafia within. The problem now is the lack of work and you will pass derelict houses and even small villages that have been abandoned. My heart goes out to the region; you just want it to work, for the situation to improve and for the people to prosper. Most Sicilians welcome you with such generosity of spirit and are keen to share with you what they have.

The island has throughout the centuries suffered appalling poverty; between 1951 and 1975, for example, one million Sicilians were forced to emigrate to the US. Those who stayed learnt to use the free and readily available ingredients around them to flavour a diet of simple grains and vegetables. Wild fennel is everywhere and mint gets trodden underfoot. I looked at some old steps in Modica and realised that, in the corner of each one, a different herb was growing. We saw mint, fennel, angelica, borage, oregano, capers – all growing wild. No wonder Sicilian food has such vibrant flavours.

Depending on where you go in Sicily you could have vastly differing opinions of the island. Most tourists will only see the manicured towns of the baroque south-east or clean and tidy Taormina, while others plump for the wild, rugged and barren coastline of the west where tourism has hardly left a mark. Palermo is not like other cities in Italy; it still has a gritty, unkempt feel in places, despite its tourist attractions. That's not to say it isn't likeable – it is, and there is plenty to do for a weekend. Just don't expect the order of Rome or the wealth of Florence. You will have great food, buzzing markets, fascinating history to discover, stunning beaches, good-value accommodation and a real and unique experience unlike anywhere else.

Having tasted the strong flavours of Sicilian produce, how, we thought, are we going to find truly Sicilian recipes that will work back home in the UK with the paltry selection of fish and forced, polytunnel-grown vegetables on offer in our local supermarket? *E fresco?* is the question you will hear your average Sicilian ask when buying fish, (bell) peppers, and, well, anything really. Sicilians are obsessed with the provenance of their food and with it being *fresco*, fresh. I just don't hear people back home saying that. We know the fish in our local store wasn't caught that morning.

The older generation still doesn't like to eat out of season. The sheer idiocy of asking for strawberries in October made our friend Mimmo, who runs his restaurant Osteria Bacchus in Sant'Ambrogio, practically hysterical. He thought it was so funny that people would come to his restaurant in autumn and ask for a strawberry sorbet – he told them to come back in June! He chuckled for ages at the ridiculous notion. As we drove away from his restaurant one chilly January day, we realised that, in the days before, we had been served strawberries at each restaurant we'd visited, even at that time of year. 'Come on Sicily,' I thought, 'stick to your roots. Don't eat food out of season; it isn't in your nature.' Now the island is covered in polytunnels to extend the season and, to my mind, that should be the only reason, to *extend* the growing season, not to go completely against nature. None of the strawberries we tasted had much flavour – better to wait for June, as Mimmo said.

One of our managers, Marianna, from our restaurant Caffè Caldesi, is Sicilian and I asked her what she was going to enjoy eating as soon as she was home for Christmas (secretly hoping for a completely original addition to my collection of Sicilian recipes). 'Ah,' she said, with a teary eye, 'fresh fish.' 'Really?' I asked. 'How will your mother cook it?' (I was still holding out hope for a secret sauce recipe passed down a long line of maternal grandmothers.) 'Simply,' she answered. 'On the outside grill, just simple; a little oil and salt, but the freshness, Katie, aah.'

Oh for goodness' sake, I wanted to cry out, they are obsessed. However, it did show me the passion for ingredients that even the young hold dear.

Seeing over the years how the Italians shop and cook, Marianna's delight at the thought of fresh fish and Mimmo's laughter at October strawberries makes me realise how important it is to get the best produce. That might mean growing what you can, choosing to shop at farmers' markets or travelling to our remaining fishmongers or independent butchers for the best and freshest ingredients. Then you keep the preparation simple; you do little to your food, but sit back and enjoy the outcome for supper. This is weekday food and the recipes we have included in our 'use three ways', which are scattered throughout the book, make the most of seasonal produce.

The exceptions to this are the complex, Arab-inspired dishes such as the sweet and sour aubergine *caponata*, pasta with sardines, pine nuts, currants and wild fennel, or couscous. These recipes are more elaborate, contain a hotchpotch of ingredients and are wonderful, but cannot be 'knocked up' in two minutes. This is our weekend way of eating, dishes that take a little longer to make but are the showstoppers.

In this series of books about the Italian regions, I have always summed up the primary ingredients in my introductions: in Amalfi it was first catch your fish, in Venice grind your spices in your pestle and mortar, in Rome it was grow your chilli and rosemary, and now in Sicily my advice would be to find lemons and oranges with leaves on to ensure their freshness.

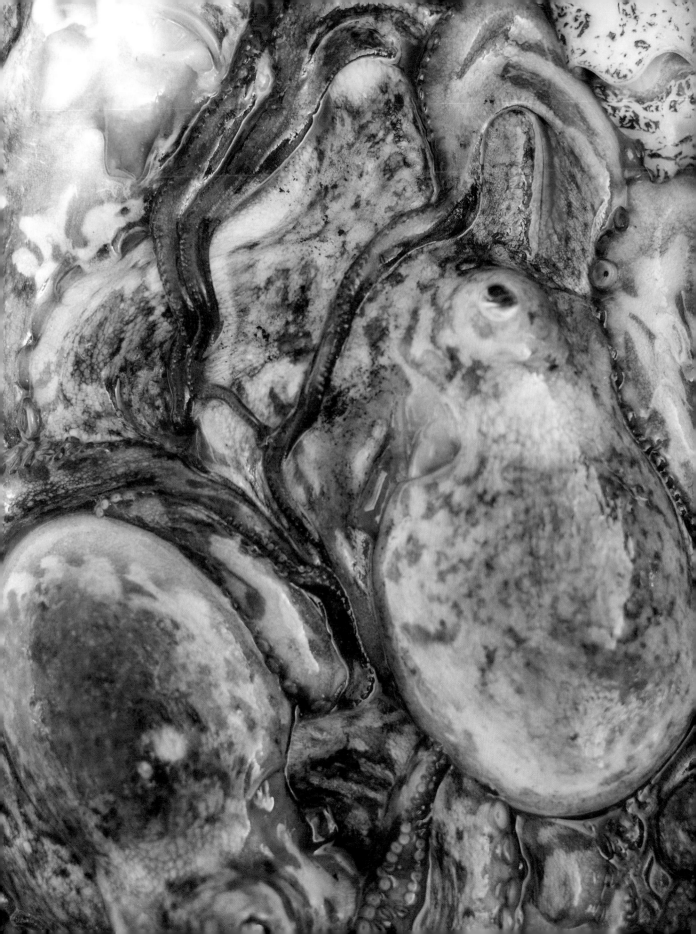

WHO BROUGHT WHAT AND 'WHEN?

For those who want to know a little more...

There are too many invasions spanning 4,000 years of Sicilian civilisation to mention here. Suffice to say that the genetic history of your average Sicilian must be fascinating to follow. You will find Sicilians of Norman descent with red hair, Greek green eyes and stature, and those from dark-skinned and dark-haired Moorish ancestry.

This is our abbreviated guide to who introduced which foodstuff to the island. It is an incredible list of diverse cultures and helps us understand why Sicilian food is so wonderfully eclectic and unlike the rest of Italy and indeed the rest of the world. Perhaps it is the first real fusion food in a land where East meets West. Eat your way around the island, sampling the dishes along the way, and you will have a lesson in its history as well as its cuisine.

Perhaps we should start with Sicily's volcano **Etna**, 500,000 years old, still growing and active today. She is said to be 'the mother that creates and destroys'. In this case she created differing microclimates around the Etna zone. When the lava flowed from the various eruptions it affected the soil – one side is perfect for pistachios and another has apples and peaches and bitter oranges. The mineral content of the soil gives the character to the produce, such as the grapes for Etna Rosso, the famous red wine from the area. Etna is one of the most active volcanoes in the world and has continued to produce a variety of minor eruptions and lava flows over the last decade.

By the 5th century BC Syracuse had become the gastronomic capital of the classical world. It was where the first school for chefs was established, and where Mithaecus wrote the **first cookbook** in the West, the *Lost Art of Cooking*.

500 K YEARS AGO · 650 BC · 350 BC

The **Greeks** arrived at Naxos in 650 BC and lived among the *Siculi* and *Sicani* and *Elymi*, the first recorded inhabitants. They built temples, many of which, like those at Agrigento and Selinunte, still exist today.

The Phoenicians, who were earlier settlers, knew how to extract a valuable purple dye by hand from the murex shellfish caught around Sicily, and built a lucrative trade across the Mediterranean. Tyrian purple was a rare and expensive dye used only for royalty.

Syracuse was founded by Greeks from Corinth and the east is still known as the Greek side. They built gardens called *horti*, where they grew grapes, olives for oil, figs, hazelnuts, walnuts and pomegranates. They used honey, made sweet wine from Malvasia grapes and ricotta from sheep and goat's milk. Seeds from carob trees were used for weighing gold. The pods were used, and still are, for cattle feed.

Around 350 BC, Archestratus, a famed Sicilian-Greek gourmet often seen as the father of gastronomy, published one of the **earliest cookbooks** under the title *Hedypatheia*, which can be translated as 'life of luxury'. He is believed to have lived in either Gela or Syracuse.

GREEK

The **Romans** won control of Sicily from the Carthaginians of North Africa in the Punic Wars of the 2nd century BC, and the island – the first Roman province outside of the Italian Peninsula – became known as the empire's granary, providing it with huge amounts of hard durum wheat and barley. The Emperor Caligula liked to hunt here on holiday from Rome. He would have enjoyed food flavoured with spices such as ginger, cinnamon, nutmeg and pepper. Salt from the salt pans of Trapani was available in Roman and Phoenician times. Cherry, plum and citron trees were imported from Asia, and 4th century AD mosaics in the Villa Romana del Casale at Piazza Armerina depict vine cultivation hunting, fishing and feasting.

In 827 AD, the **Saracens** from North Africa invaded and took the west coast, which is still known as the Arab side. Arab culture is evident to this day in the language, architecture and food. In 1154 AD the Arab geographer al-Idrisi wrote a document for the Norman king of Sicily, Roger II, which mentions *itriyya* – a type of **pasta** introduced into Sicily from Palestine by the **Arabs** and produced and exported in huge quantities from Norman Sicily. There are documents dating from 1371 that reveal that the prices of macaroni and lasagne in Palermo were triple those of bread. It was a food enjoyed mostly by the aristocracy and by the Jewish population, because pasta came to be taxed in the 15th century. Pasta strands were originally eaten with the hands but the addition of sauces led to the widespread use of the table fork. Couscous, another food brought to Sicily by the Arabs, is still found along the west coast.

The first Jews came to Sicily with the Greeks, and by the time of the Middle Ages they had become a rich elite. The second influx was of Jews escaping from the Spanish Inquisition at the end of the 15th century, but then many had to flee again when the Inquisition reached Sicily, although a large number stayed behind and converted to Christianity. The Jews did not eat certain parts of the animal, so they gave these scraps to the poor Christians. The Catholics of Palermo used these scraps to create street food, which they relish to this day, made exclusively of offal, such as *milza* (spleen) and *stigghiole*, the intestines of a young cow, lamb or goat.

200 BC · 535 AD · 807 · 827 · 902

In 535 AD Sicily became part of the **Byzantine Empire** following the break-up of the Roman Empire.

In 807 AD, the North African Arabs introduced the *mattanza*, the tuna cull, using a sophisticated system of nets. It became embedded in Sicilian culture. The Arabs brought new methods of agriculture, including terracing and aqueducts for irrigation. Sicily grew into a major exporter and trading centre. Muslim, Christian and Jewish traders crowded the markets of Palermo.

In 902 AD, the Arabs began to plant almonds, sugarcane, citrus, rice, bananas, mulberries, aubergines, date palms, pistachios, watermelons and apricots. Pine nuts, garlic and saffron were often included in dishes for their flavour but they were also thought to possess antibacterial properties. Sesame seeds were added to bread.

Snow and fruit was mixed to make *sherbets*, an early type of sorbet flavoured with rose and jasmine, still popular flavours today. You can see the modern version of this in the popular *granite* served in a bun for breakfast.

The Arabs combined sugar, ricotta, nuts and fruits to make sweets, a mixture that still fills the ubiquitous *cannoli* and *cassata* found all over the island. The Christians later absorbed this knowledge and patisserie produced in the convents and monasteries was given religious significance.

Arab meals comprised one course, unlike the Roman fashion for several. Substantial one-plate meals such as the couscous on page 163 and baked rice dishes like the *timballo* on page 158 were introduced.

ROMAN/ BYZANTINE

ARAB

The **Norman conquest** began in 1060, led by the brothers Robert and Roger Hauteville. They were descendants of the Vikings from Scandinavia and they were ruthless warriors, certainly not men known for their erudition. E. Joranson, in his book about the Norman conquests of Southern Italy, described what the brothers might have found: 'Lemons, almonds, pickled nuts, fine vestments and iron instruments chased with gold; and thus they tempted them to come to this land that flows with milk and honey and with so many beautiful things.'

The Pope offered Robert the dukedoms of Apulia, Calabria and Sicily, where the Byzantines were trying to re-establish their rule over the Arabs. By 1091 the Normans had the whole of Sicily and the Calabrian peninsula under their control. Although the brothers overthrew the Arabs, Roger as Great Count of Sicily embraced much of their culture in setting up his Arab-Norman empire. The Arab influence probably brought little to the culinary landscape other than their salt cod, known as *baccalà*, but most importantly, they didn't destroy it either. Valentina, our guide around historic Palermo, told us that generally the Sicilians don't like to destroy; instead, they prefer to add to what is already there. You can see this in the architecture as well as the food. Roger's son ruled as Roger II from 1101 and left a legacy of acceptance of other cultures. He spoke Arabic, French, Latin and Greek, created the spectacular Palatine Chapel and hired Arab chefs to cook for his court. The court of King Roger has been described by one historian as 'by far the most brilliant of twelfth-century Europe'.

1492: When the Jews were expelled from Sicily by the Inquisition, they fled to Rome and elsewhere around the world, taking their traditions with them. Among these was the art, learnt from the Arabs, of frying small pieces of cheap food to sell as street food to the Romans. The Jews introduced the use of currants and pine nuts and aubergines (eggplants) to Rome. The Romans named the weird purple vegetable the *mela insana*, 'mad apple'. The modern word is *melanzane*. The sugar industry in Sicily was run mainly by the Jews, who made vast fortunes from trading through the spice routes using their connections from Damascus to Venice – until their expulsion brought this to an abrupt end.

1535: Pastry making took hold in the convents and monasteries. After the 1600s, agriculture yields and exports plummeted and Sicily fell into a decline.

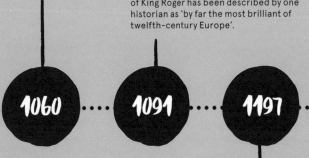

| 1060 | 1091 | 1197 | 1302 | 1500 | 1535 |

The famous Sicilian painted carts originated in the time of Emperor Frederick II, grandson of Roger II, who became King of Sicily in 1197 following the end of the Norman dynasty. (He was King of Sicily from 1197 to 1250, crowned King of Germany in 1212 and Holy Roman Emperor in 1217.) The highly coloured carts, used to transport oranges and lemons, were decorated with religious scenes but also Arabic patterns for festivals, a tradition that continued until the 1970s when motor vehicles took over. During this period, the school of Sicilian poetry was formed. French influences in cooking could be seen at this time. Rolled meat such as the *Rotolo di Farsumagru* on page 175 was invented after the French *roulé*.

In 1302, the **Spanish nobles** arrived and brought pumpkins, tomatoes and peppers. Today the area of Pachino still grows tons of tomatoes. They are sold as they are or dried in the sun or reduced and concentrated to make *estrattu*, the extract of tomato which is sold by weight at markets from a pile of dark red paste. The prickly pear cactus, known as Indian figs or *fiche d'India*, was brought from Mexico to Sicily by ship. They are still popular today, brightly coloured fruits that are sold whole or ready peeled.

Cocoa beans and the Aztec method of making them into chocolate were brought to Modica by the Spanish. A specifically Sicilian form of chocolate is still produced there in the same way today (see page 209).

Cooking in the aristocratic houses of the Spanish nobility from the early 1500s, often referred to as *cucina baronale*, baronial cooking, flourished up until the middle of the 20th century. It signalled the beginning of the huge divide between the rich and poor with almost nothing in between. Many of the Sicilian dishes we know today were originally made to copy what the wealthy were eating during this time. Instead of a dish of meat slow-cooked in wine, the Sicilian poor would eat Romanesco cauliflower in wine, and *caponata* was a sweet and sour sauce originally for fish but the poor made it with aubergine instead. The cooking of the poor was known as *cucina povera*.

NORMAN

SPANISH

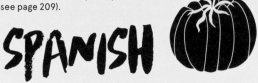

1713: The Duke of Savoy took over Sicily under the terms of the Treaty of Utrecht, which ended the European-wide War of the Spanish Succession, subsequently ceding the kingdom to the Austrians a few years later.

1734: The Bourbon Charles III took the throne for Spain. Ferdinand I, son of Charles III, inherited the throne of Sicily in 1767 and ruled from Naples.

1789, Palermo: Goethe declared, 'Italy without Sicily cannot be conceived; here is the key to everything.' In his *Italian Journey* he said, 'To have seen Italy without seeing Sicily is not to have seen Italy at all, for Sicily is the clue to everything.'

1816: The kingdoms of Sicily and Naples were united to form the Kingdom of the Two Sicilies.

In the 1880s the growth of the Mafia across much of rural Sicily was greatly assisted by the development of the lemon trade, which became of strategic importance to the Sicilian economy. The high profits from this industry were targeted by the Mafia in return for 'protection'.

1713 1773 1789 1805 1860 1880 1943–

In 1773, John Woodhouse, an Englishman with experience of the fortified wines of Spain and Portugal, invented marsala, the fortified wine made principally from the local grillo, inzolia or catarratto grapes to which grape spirit or brandy is added. Marsala is used for savoury and sweet dishes. The revictualling of Admiral Nelson's fleet off Syracuse in 1798, prior to his victory over the French in the battle of the Nile, helped to spread the popularity of the wine.

In 1805, the Royal Court relocated to Palermo under King Ferdinand IV. His wife was Maria Carolina, sister of Marie Antoinette. Maria brought her French chef to the court in 1805. Others followed and became known as the *monzù*, from the word *monsieur*. The term was used only to describe French chefs but was later extended to the local Sicilians and Neapolitans who had worked under them. They made more delicate *arancine*, more like canapés. The desserts developed during this time were influenced by the cooking of northern Italy and France and based on chocolate, pastry, cream and butter.

The Leopard by Giuseppe Tomasi di Lampedusa was set at this time and describes grand feasts and the delights cooked by the *monzù*, including rum jelly and macaroni pie.

In 1860 Garibaldi and his 'redshirts' began their campaign for the unification of Italy in Sicily and oust the Spanish. The Sicilians voted almost unanimously for this new government of all Italy, thereby bringing to an end the rule of the Bourbons. Naples followed suit five months later and in 1861 the whole of Italy became unified.

In 1943, American forces (under General Patton in the west of Sicily) and British forces (under General Montgomery in the east) forces invaded and threw out the remaining Fascists and Germans with the help of the Mafia.

1999: The television series *Montalbano*, filmed in Modica, helped to revive the tourist industry of the south-east of the island.

ITALIAN

PALERMO & ITS STREET FOOD

PALERMO & ITS STREET FOOD

From slices of bright red and green watermelon sold to refresh you in summer, to hot salt-baked chestnuts and the curls of white smoke emanating from their stalls in winter, there is always something to tempt you on the streets of Palermo.

Street food dates back at least to Roman times and possibly before. For centuries people had no ovens at home and fuel was short, so hot food would only have been available on the street. We decided to take a food tour around the capital. It was years since we had been to Palermo and all I remember from the last time is running away from drug dealers I had inadvertently filmed on a small video camera at the edge of Ballarò market. Such was my wonder at the place, the dilapidated buildings, a shadow of their former grandness, the beguiling smiles and cheerful shouting of the market stallholders bragging about their best produce. Palermo is gritty, visceral and edgy. And the produce against this backdrop? Such perfect tomatoes, bumpy skinned, ripe and colourful; huge distorted (bell) peppers; celery with leaves you can smell as you pass, bright freshly caught fish often still alive or in rigor, courgettes (zucchini) in all shapes and sizes – nothing uniform for the supermarket, each piece unique.

Our guide to the street food of Palermo was Salvatore Agusta, who runs tours around his city. Sicily has the right climate for street food and enough poor people and now inquisitive tourists to demand it. He told us there are five key points to street food:

- It is soft – so it is easy to eat with no cutlery (and possibly, in the past, few teeth).
- It has few ingredients – five or six max, so it doesn't take too much time or money to make.
- It must be cheap and is usually made or coated with filling carbohydrate.
- It has a historical connotation – each type of street food tells a story of the past.
- It is fresh – the food is usually sold very soon after the final step in making it, which might be frying it off or putting the meat in the bun.

'Fry shops', or *friggitorie*, sell *panelle* – chickpea fritters – as well as hot battered vegetables and potato *crocchè*. Ready-cooked food such as boiled potatoes, roasted onions in their skins and blackened peppers can be eaten straight away or taken home to make into a salad. Slices of soft, squashy bread topped with tomato and onion sauce known as *sfincione* are so good, not to mention everyone's favourite – the *arancine*, rice balls.

Less tempting perhaps to our palates are the various stalls selling fried and boiled entrails from one animal or another. The Palermitani absolutely love these. Pippo, from the aptly named stall Joie, told me, 'It's good what you like, it is no good what is beautiful.' He has to say this, I feel, as the bowl of boiled entrails, *bollito*, is probably the least pretty food I have ever seen. Giancarlo was salivating at the thought of tasting spleen again, a food memory from his childhood in Tuscany. I did try it, and actually found it pleasant; each of the organ meats had its own texture and flavour and I agree we should eat all parts of the animal. It was an interesting experience: the brain was soft and had a flavour of corned beef; the milky entrails fought back a little; the foot was chewy; the udder was like a squashy, rough paste and the tongue grainy and soft. I was rewarded by Pippo for my bravery with a cold glass of Nero d'Avola (the best bit) and I was proud of having given it a go. The locals, he told me, take home 1.5 kg (3 lb) bags of boiled organ meat to make salad, which is enough to feed a family of ten.

On another trip around the market our guide Vincenzo insisted I try *frittola* – scraps of meat, scraped off the bone and fried in lard – *stigghiole*, the intestines of a young cow, lamb or goat; and *pani ca meuza*, a soft bun filled with boiled spleen and a squeeze of lemon.

Veal spleen in a bun is famous in Palermo and has a Jewish history. The Jews were allowed to work with metal and kill animals but the Torah prevented them from taking money for it. They did, however, take the interior meat as payment, known as the fifth quarter. They then boiled parts of this in lard and sold it back to the Palermitani. The pan was originally boiled over coals at an angle so that the fat drains to one side. The Jews were expelled by the Spanish following the edict of 1492 and local Palermitani took over running the stands, a tradition carried on by men like Guiseppe Basile, whom we met on our tour, and whose family has been doing it for generations.

There are two main markets in Palermo: Ballarò and Capo. The previously large market of Vucciria (named after the French for butcher's, *boucherie*) is a shadow of its former self. Still now, *troppo Vucciria* means 'too much noise', harking back to when it was a thriving butchers' area.

ARANCINE

The word *arancine* comes from the Italian for oranges since they are the same colour and shape. They have been made in various forms since the days of Arab rule and were made originally by the Tuareg, the pastoral nomads, with goat meat and couscous. It was the chef of Frederick II who replaced the couscous with rice so that the *arancine* held together better. Saffron was added as it was thought to make them last longer. *Arancine* were taken on hunting expeditions by the aristocracy so that they could eat without having to light a fire and thus draw attention to themselves. The chef also covered them in egg and breadcrumbs to provide further protection and it is this coating that gives the *arancine* their crunch. In this way, they are similar to Cornish pasties, as you were supposed to eat just the inside and discard the crust, which was dirty from being handled. The Sicilians have a particular kind of rice for this – an old variety that becomes sticky when cooked. They use the same rice in Spain for paella.

In Palermo, the different flavours are denoted by the shapes: the cones are spinach, the rounds are mushroom, the oblongs are mozzarella and ham, and the balls are the original one, the ragu. They are huge and one is enough for a whole meal. In eastern Sicily, around Catania, the *arancine* have a more conical shape, reminiscent of Mount Etna. When the Spanish came they brought their French chefs, the *monzù*, and they made more delicate *arancine*, more like canapés.

The ragu in *arancine* is a little like the filling for cottage pie. It has minced (ground) meat, carrots, tomatoes and onions and is a little spicy. It contains a full-bodied red wine such as the typical Sicilian Nero d'Avola and lots of black pepper. The béchamel is a binder and helps the ragu hold together. Do play around with the flavours but a little béchamel is always a good idea. Here we have made one batch and split it in half for two different flavours. The rice in Palermo is yellow with saffron and has no tomatoes in it. Good *arancine* should have a lot of stuffing. The breadcrumbs should be fine and ideally the balls should be fried in lard, but seed oil is a good replacement.

Flavours are open to the imagination or what you have left over in the fridge. At the recently opened Ke Palle, a shop devoted to *arancine* in Via Maqueda, Palermo, you will find everything from pistachio, stracchino and speck to prawn (shrimp), spinach and ricotta, and even sweet ones filled with Nutella or pistachio cream.

ARANCINE

**Makes approximately 10 *arancine*
7 cm (2¾ in) wide**

500 g (1 lb 2 oz/2¼ cups) Arborio rice
salt
½–1 teaspoon saffron strands, depending
on your taste
50 g (2 oz/½ stick) salted butter
seed oil for frying

For the béchamel
(half for the ragu and half for the ham
and cheese)
400 ml (13 fl oz/1¾ cups) whole milk
1 bay leaf
75 g (2½ oz/generous ¼ cup) salted
butter
60 g (2 oz/½ cup) '00' flour or cornflour
salt and freshly ground black pepper
good pinch of ground nutmeg

For the mozzarella and ham filling
150 g (5 oz) cooked ham, finely chopped
120 g (4 oz) mozzarella, finely chopped
15 g (½ oz) Parmesan, finely grated
75 g (2½ oz/scant ½ cup) cooked
petits pois

For the ragu filling
250 g (9 oz) cooked and cooled Quick
Beef Ragu (see page 131)

For the coating
100 g (3½ oz/1 cup) '00' flour or gluten-
free flour
150 ml (5 fl oz/⅔ cup) tepid water
100 g (3½ oz/1 cup) fine dry breadcrumbs
(you can use gluten-free)

Cook the rice in plenty of lightly salted water for 17–20 minutes or until soft. Remove from the heat and drain, keeping a little of the cooking water. Mix the saffron with a couple of tablespoons of the starchy rice cooking water and stir into the rice with the butter. Taste the rice and adjust the salt and saffron flavours as necessary. Pour into an open wide bowl and allow the rice to cool quickly. Don't keep it out of the fridge for any longer than 1 hour.

To make the béchamel, warm the milk with the bay leaf in a saucepan over a medium heat. Warm the butter and flour in another saucepan and stir to combine. Let the flour mixture bubble a little in the pan then pour into the hot milk and immediately whisk through, keeping the pan over the heat. Season with salt, pepper and nutmeg. When the sauce starts to thicken, remove the pan from the heat and divide between two bowls, discarding the bay leaf. Cover both with cling film (plastic wrap) touching the surface and allow to cool. When cold, stir the ham, cheeses and peas into one bowl, and the ragu into the other.

Make the coating by mixing the flour with the water and blending until smooth with a whisk or a stick blender. Set aside in a bowl large enough to dip in the *arancine*. Put the breadcrumbs into a separate bowl.

Work the rice through with your hands, squeezing and breaking down the grains, for around 5 minutes (it's actually quite therapeutic and enjoyable!). If you dip your hands in cold water first, the rice will stick less. Weigh out around 120 g (4 oz) of rice and flatten it a little into the palm of your hand. Make a small well in the centre. Put around 30 g (1 oz) of either the ragu or the cheese and ham mixture into the hollow, then close the rice around it, squeezing and pushing the rice together into a ball in your palms. Dip the *arancina* into the batter and, as you bring it out, let the batter drain off. Now roll it in the breadcrumbs. Pick up more breadcrumbs and scatter them over, lightly pressing them into the surface. Put the *arancine* straight into hot oil to fry, or finish making them all before cooking. At this point they can be frozen, but should be defrosted in a fridge overnight before cooking.

To fry them, heat the oil in a deep-sided saucepan or a deep-fat fryer to around 175°C (347°F) and fry the *arancine* for 5–7 minutes, or until they turn a deep orangey-brown. Use a skewer to pierce the *arancine* through to the centre and pull them out of the oil. Touch the tip of the skewer to see if it is hot. If it isn't, cook the balls for longer. Drain on kitchen paper and eat straight away.

SPINACH & MOZZARELLA ARANCINE

For the filling
150 g (5 oz) cooked and squeezed-out spinach
2 tablespoons extra-virgin olive oil
1 garlic clove, peeled and lightly crushed
salt and freshly ground black pepper
120 g (4 oz) mozzarella, roughly chopped
50 g (2 oz) Parmesan, finely grated
¼ teaspoon ground nutmeg, to taste

Sauté the cooked spinach in the oil with the garlic and seasoning for a few minutes. Remove from the heat, discard the garlic and finely chop the spinach. Put into a bowl and, when cool, add the remaining ingredients and stir to combine. Fill and cook your *arancine* as on page 24.

MINI CRAB ARANCINE

These are pop-in-your-mouth, all-in-one-go sized rice balls that are perfect for a party. Prepare them in advance and keep them in the fridge, then fry or oven bake the *arancine* at the last minute to serve warm to guests. By dipping them in batter and breadcrumbs they will form a crispy coating which is lovely around the soft rice centres. For ease, especially when entertaining, you can simply oven bake the *arancine*. We serve these as amuse-bouches at our restaurant Caldesi in Campagna, where instead of crab we often mix the rice with truffle oil, cooked porcini mushrooms or simply lots of finely grated cheese and chopped herbs. You can also make them with leftover risotto.

Makes 30 walnut-sized *arancine*

½ quantity of the rice (250 g/9 oz/ generous 1 cup) cooked and mixed with saffron and butter as the recipe for *Arancine* on page 24
300 g (10½ oz) white crab meat (or a mixture of brown and white crab meat)
large handful of parsley, finely chopped
salt and freshly ground black pepper
seed oil for frying or extra-virgin olive oil for brushing

Preheat the oven to 180°C (350°F/Gas 4). Once the rice has cooled, mix in the crab meat, parsley and seasoning and form 20 walnut-sized balls. Now either dip them in the batter and breadcrumbs as in the *Arancine* recipe on page 24, or simply brush them with a little olive oil and put them on a lightly oiled baking tray. Bake in the oven for 15–20 minutes or until hot and the oil is slightly bubbling at the sides.

CHICKPEA FRITTERS

If you wander around any market in Sicily you will see *panelle*, meaning 'little breads', for sale. These chickpea fritters are often served in a bun – so it will be *pane e panelle*. *Panelle* are made from pouring chickpea (gram) flour into boiling water with salt and sometimes herbs. They are cooked in vats of bubbling oil for just a few minutes. Tipping them onto a marble slab (not wood as it is absorbent) means they cool quickly on the cold surface.

Serves 6–8

2 tablespoons extra-virgin olive oil
300 g (10½ oz/3¼ cups) chickpea
   (gram) flour
1 teaspoon salt
900 ml (31 fl oz/4 cups) water
15 g (½ oz) parsley or celery leaves,
   or 2 teaspoons fennel seeds,
   lightly crushed
seed oil for deep-frying

Brush a standard shallow oven tray with a tablespoon of the olive oil and set aside. Brush the remaining olive oil over a piece of baking parchment the same size as the tray and set aside. Put the flour, salt and water into a saucepan and whisk together well. Put the pan on to the heat and bring to the boil, whisking continuously. When the mixture starts to thicken and splutter remove from the heat and add the parsley or fennel seeds. Pour the mixture on to the baking tray and cover with the oily side of the baking parchment. Press it down all over so that you have an even layer of chickpea batter around 5 mm (¼ in) thick.

Remove the parchment and set the tray aside to cool and the mixture to set for 30–40 minutes. Cut the cooled mixture into squares approximately 5 x 5 cm (2 x 2 in) for traditional *panelle*. Heat the oil in a large saucepan or a deep-fat fryer to 175°C (347°F) or hot enough to brown a small piece of bread instantly. Fry the fritters for about 5 minutes or until golden brown on all sides. Drain on kitchen paper and sprinkle with a little salt before serving while still warm.

OVEN—BAKED RICOTTA WITH ONIONS & ROSEMARY

We saw this dish in Ballarò market in Palermo, where a father and son were a wonderful double act, calling out for people to come and admire their cheese stall. They had every imaginable local cheese on offer, as well as a few inventions of the father. He took great pride in asking me to come and see his tiny oven where he was baking fresh ricotta. The smell alone of roasting onions and rosemary was enough to draw a crowd. It seemed such a simple idea I couldn't wait to get home to try it. It's brilliant and a recipe I keep returning to when I have people coming round. Serve the ricotta hot from the oven with one of the focaccia recipes on pages 37–38 – it is lovely like this and even more special with the Sun-dried Tomato & Chilli Relish on page 59.

Serves 4–6 as antipasti

---

250 g (9 oz/1 cup) ricotta
salt and freshly ground black pepper
3 sprigs of rosemary, needles removed
  from the stems
1 shallot, finely chopped
3 tablespoons extra-virgin olive oil

Preheat the oven to 180°C (350°F/Gas 4) and line a baking tray with baking parchment (I tear a piece so that it has rough edges and serve the ricotta on a wooden board on the paper, as it browns lightly in the oven). Drain the ricotta by tipping out any water from the container and turn it out onto the baking tray. Gently make a dip in the top of the cheese and scatter over the seasoning, rosemary and chopped shallot, piling it up on top. Pour over the oil and bake for 20–30 minutes or until lightly browned. Serve with crusty bread.

Use 3 Ways

On pizza, Baked
Sea bass (see
page 204), pasta

SICILIAN PIZZA

Sfincione is a squashy Sicilian deep pizza topped with a delicious oniony tomato sauce. This is lovely on its own and is eaten in Palermo as a snack or with a buffet of antipasti. It is thought that the Sicilians who moved to the US took the idea of this deep-dish-style pizza with them. The topping varies from town to town around the island; sometimes there are no tomatoes, sometimes the pizza is covered in *primosale*, a young fresh sheep's cheese, or breadcrumbs and grated Parmesan. The sauce makes more than you need, but it's so delicious you can eat it stirred into pasta, on cooked fish or on the Quick Ricotta Sfincione on page 37. In the photo, the pizza is served with the Focaccia from page 38.

Serves 4–6

For the dough
250 g (9 oz/2 cups) '00' flour
7 g (¼ oz) fresh yeast or 3 g
   (1 heaped teaspoon) fast-action
   dried yeast
1 teaspoon fine salt
225 ml (8 fl oz/1 cup) tepid water
5 tablespoons extra-virgin olive oil

For the *sfincione* sauce
1 large onion, cut in half from root to tip
   and thinly sliced into half-moons
3 tablespoons extra-virgin olive oil
4 anchovies in oil, drained
freshly ground black pepper
1 x 400 g tin chopped tomatoes
1 tablespoon tomato purée
   (tomato paste)
1 teaspoon dried oregano
25 g (1 oz) Parmesan, finely grated

Mix the flour, yeast, salt, water and 2 tablespoons of the oil in a mixer with a whisk attachment at a medium speed or an electric whisk for 10 minutes. Use a tablespoon of the oil to thoroughly grease a 23–25 cm (9–10 in) round tin and pour in the dough. Pour the remaining oil over the whole surface so that the dough can rise in the tin but won't dry out. You can spread the dough with your fingers if you dip them in oil first. Leave in a warm place to rise and double in volume. This could take anywhere between 1–2 hours, depending on the warmth of the room. The slower the rise, the better the flavour and larger the holes in the bread, so it is better not to rush it. You will know the dough is ready when you press an oiled finger into the surface and it returns back to shape slowly.

Meanwhile, fry the onion in the oil over a low heat with the anchovies and a little black pepper until soft and slightly caramelised. This will take up to 15 minutes – you don't want the onion to take on any colour but you want the sweetness to come through. Add the tomatoes, tomato purée and oregano and stir through. Bring to the boil then simmer for 40 minutes over a medium heat to allow the sauce to reduce. Transfer to a bowl to cool.

Preheat the oven to 200°C (400°F/Gas 6). When the dough is swollen, gently pour over approximately 150 g (5 oz) of the sauce. Transfer the bread to the oven and bake for 20 minutes. Scatter over the cheese and continue to bake for a further 5–10 minutes or until the sauce has started to brown around the edges and the cheese has melted. Take out of the oven and remove from the tin straight away. Allow to cool on a rack.

QUICK RICOTTA SFINCIONE

This is another brilliant idea from the man at the cheese stall at Ballarò market in Palermo and it makes a lovely quick lunch or snack if you already have the *sfincione* sauce. Instead of making the dough for a pizza, take a piece of sourdough bread and smear it with a thick layer of ricotta. Spread over a generous spoonful of *sfincione* sauce (see page 35) and scatter over a pinch of dried oregano. Cook for 10–15 minutes at 180°C (350°F/Gas 4) or until lightly browned.

SICILIAN FOCACCIA WITH SESAME SEEDS

Follow the recipe for Sicilian Pizza on page 35, scattering 2 teaspoons each of dried oregano and sesame seeds over the surface of the dough before it rises and omitting the *sfincione* sauce. Cook as the Sicilian Pizza for 20–25 minutes. See photo on page 34.

GLUTEN-FREE FOCACCIA

After much experimentation we are really happy with this nutty focaccia. It even has the typically big holes of traditional focaccia. We love the flavour of chestnut flour; it offers sweetness to the dough and deepens the colour. However, if you can't find it, substitute it with extra gluten-free flour instead. This recipe can be used to make either the Sicilian Pizza on page 35 or the Sicilian Focaccia with Sesame Seeds on page 37.

Serves 6–8

200 g (7 oz/1⅔ cups) gluten-free flour
50 g (2 oz/generous ½ cup) chestnut flour
7 g (¼ oz) fresh yeast or 3 g (1 heaped teaspoon)
    fast-action dried yeast
1 heaped teaspoon xantham gum
1 teaspoon fine salt
225 ml (8 fl oz/1 cup) tepid water
2 eggs
3 tablespoons extra-virgin olive oil
2 teaspoons sesame seeds
2 teaspoons dried oregano

Mix the flours, yeast, xantham gum, salt, water, eggs and 1 tablespoon of the oil in a mixer with a whisk attachment at a medium speed or an electric whisk for 10 minutes. Use a little of the remaining oil to thoroughly grease a 23–25 cm (9–10 in) round tin and pour in the dough. Pour the rest of the oil over the whole surface so that the dough can rise in the tin but won't dry out. You can spread the oil with your fingers if you dip them in oil first. Scatter over the sesame seeds and oregano. Leave in a warm place to rise and double in volume. This could take anywhere between 1–2 hours, depending on the warmth of the room.

Preheat the oven to 200°C (400°F/Gas 6). Transfer the bread to the oven and bake for 20 minutes. Take out of the oven and remove from the tin straight away. Put back into the oven on a rack for 5 minutes to cook through. Remove from the oven and allow to cool on a rack.

Variation: To make this gluten-free focaccia into the Sicilian Pizza, follow the instructions on page 35 adding the *sfincione* sauce and cheese. When it is cooked, remove it from the tin and give it 5 more minutes in the oven on a rack to ensure it is cooked through.

ROUND SANDWICHES

All around the island, round, flattish loaves such as Monreale bread, sesame seeded loaves or simple focaccia are split in half and filled with the most delicious combinations. These 'sandwiches' used to be poor man's food and could be taken to the fields for lunch. Now cafés and wine bars such as the Enoteca Rossorubino in Cefalù serve them cut into wedges with wonderful local wines and olives.

Here, Francsco and Mimmo from Osteria Bacchus in Sant'Ambrogio showed us their favourite combination of sliced tomatoes, mozzarella, lettuce, anchovies broken into pieces and smeared over the bread, oregano, pepper and salt. It is important that the bread is not too hard to bite through and it should be moistened with good olive oil and sliced tomatoes. Or try tinned sardines, a few anchovies, plenty of chopped parsley and lemon juice or soft goat's cheese, sliced tomatoes, rocket (arugula) leaves and the Sun-dried Tomato & Chilli Relish on page 59.

SCACCE

As our friend Anne Hudson pointed out when we made these together, every culture has a version of pastry wrapped around a filling, usually developed to eat as food on the run. Think of the Cornish pasty, the Indian samosa, the French crêpe or the Mexican burrito. It's a great way to use up leftovers such as cooked sausage with onions, roasted vegetables and ricotta or sautéed mushrooms with cheese and thyme. Our favourite flavour while experimenting was smoked cheese with the Cherry Tomato Sauce on page 144. *Scacce*, although available in a couple of shops in Palermo, are not from the same area. They originate in the south-east of the island and are typical of the pretty town of Modica. The recipe makes enough for two long rolls of *scacce*. We have given the ingredients to make two different fillings. *Scacce* keep well in a sealed bag in the fridge and are great to take on picnics.

> **Serves 4 as a main course**
> **or 6 as a starter**

For the dough
250 g (9 oz/2 cups) '00' flour, plus extra
    for dusting or 250 g (9 oz/2 cups)
    gluten-free flour and 1 teaspoon
    xanthan gum
3.5 g (1 heaped teaspoon) dried active
    yeast
1 teaspoon salt
150 ml (5 fl oz/⅔ cup) tepid water
1 tablespoon plus 2 teaspoons extra
    virgin olive oil

Roast aubergine and ricotta filling
250 g (9 oz/1 cup) ricotta
100 g (3½ oz) roast aubergine (eggplant)
    (see page 138) or half the Roast
    Peppers recipe (see page 96)
small handful of torn basil leaves
25 g (1 oz) Parmesan (if not using the
    Palermitana recipe), grated
salt and freshly ground black pepper
1 tablespoon extra-virgin olive oil,
    to drizzle over

**Cherry tomato and smoked cheese
filling**
150 g (5 oz) Cherry Tomato Sauce
    (see page 144)
50 g (2 oz) smoked cheese, grated
1 x 125 g (4 oz) ball of mozzarella, torn
    into shreds
1 teaspoon dried oregano
salt and freshly ground black pepper
2 tablespoons extra-virgin olive oil,
    to drizzle over

Put all of the dry ingredients for the dough into the bowl of a mixer and, using a dough hook, blend together (or do this by hand in a bowl). Add 1 tablespoon of the olive oil followed by the water, a little at a time, until you have a soft, pliable dough that leaves the sides of the bowl clean. You may not need all of the water – it depends upon the absorbency of the flour. If you are making a gluten-free version, be prepared to add a little more water as necessary. Continue to knead in the mixer or by hand for 5 minutes. Lightly oil a bowl with 1 teaspoon of the olive oil, and transfer the ball of dough to it. Cover with cling film (plastic wrap) and leave to rise for approximately 1–1½ hours at room temperature, or until doubled in size.

Preheat the oven to 200°C (400°F/Gas 6) and grease a baking tray with 1 teaspoon of the olive oil. Divide the dough in half and roll each half out on a floured work surface to a rectangle roughly 50 cm (20 in) long and 30 cm (12 in) wide. It should be just transparent. Patch up any holes or the filling will come out. Use the rolling pin to help lift both halves, each one onto a floured tea towel.

Use one filling for one dough half, and the other filling for the second one. Evenly spread the filling ingredients over the dough, starting with either the ricotta or the Cherry Tomato Sauce and layering up the rest of the ingredients, leaving a border of around 2 cm (¾ in) clear around the edges. Drizzle the olive oil over the filling and fold in the clean edges. Lift one long edge of the tea towel and roll up the pastry like a fat, slightly flattened Swiss roll and place on the baking tray. It should be around 6 cm (2½ in) wide. Wipe the surface with the remaining oil using your fingers. Put into the oven straight away and bake for 35 minutes. Remove from the oven and allow to cool a little before eating. It can be cooled completely and eaten cold, but it never makes it to that stage in our house – it's just too tempting.

ANTIPASTI

ANTIPASTI

In the market in Ortigia I met an Australian woman enjoying a late breakfast of a glass of mellow white wine and a board of antipasti: tiny samples of the local food, such as *caponata*, the sweet and sour vegetable dish served in various guises all over the island, accompanied by *panelle* (the Chickpea Fritters on page 28), locally sun-dried tomatoes, olives, sliced meats and cheeses, and, typically, a hunk of Sicilian Focaccia with Sesame Seeds (see page 37). The idea of eating several dishes at one sitting dates back to Roman times in Sicily and has changed little since.

SARDINE PATTIES

During the period of the Bourbons, the Sicilian people couldn't afford meat and substituted fish for the meat in meatballs. Actually, it was probably far healthier than the meat version and full of nutritious omega-3 fatty acids and vitamins. Sardine patties are great for party canapés, served at room temperature with a squeeze of lemon just before serving. Alternatively, they can be made into the size of small hamburgers and served warm with the Orange & Fennel Salad on page 111, the Sweet & Sour Onions on page 199 or in the Cherry Tomato Sauce on page 144 as a starter or main course. Traditionally, they are deep-fried but they work well fried in just a little oil in a non-stick frying pan; or you could bake them in the oven to be healthier. Don't be put off using tinned sardines – they are as healthy as fresh and a great way to use this inexpensive source of protein.

Makes approximately 35 patties

---

15 small fresh sardines (approximately 900 g/2 lb total weight) or 4 x 120 g tins sardines

1 small onion, grated

100 g (3½ oz/1¼ cups) fresh gluten-free or wheat breadcrumbs

2 tablespoons juicy sweet currants or raisins

3 tablespoons pine nuts

large handful of mint leaves, finely chopped

large handful of parsley, finely chopped

1 heaped teaspoon salt and a good twist of freshly ground black pepper

3 tablespoons white wine or sweet marsala

3 tablespoons extra-virgin olive oil

seed oil for frying or extra-virgin olive oil for brushing if baking

Cut the flesh of the fresh sardines into small pieces no bigger than 5 mm (¼ in), discarding the spines and heads. If using tinned, drain them and roughly mash with a fork. Mix the sardines with the rest of the ingredients (except the seed oil or olive oil for brushing).

Test the flavour of the patties by making just one to begin with. Form the mixture into a ball in your hands, approximately 3 cm (1¼ in) across. Flatten it slightly and fry it in a little oil on both sides until lightly golden and cooked through. Taste and adjust the seasoning and flavours of the remaining mixture as necessary. Make up the rest of the patties and fry in batches in more oil as before.

To cook them in the oven, space them out on a baking tray lined with baking parchment and brush with a little olive oil. Bake in a preheated oven at 180°C (350°F/Gas 4) for 15–20 minutes or until cooked through.

ARTICHOKE BROAD BEAN & HERB CASSEROLE

This is a lovely traditional dish made with the small fresh artichokes of spring, the first broad (fava) beans and peas of the year and wild herbs from the fields. Since we just can't get the same artichokes here I use tinned or jarred artichokes and rinse them before use. If you are thinking of cheating, do use frozen peas and broad beans. The beans are frozen when young and tender and don't need their shells removed. Do add the full handful of herbs – the flavours are wonderful and it changes the dish according to what you have. Although we have included this in the Antipasti section, it also makes a good vegetarian or vegan lunch (if you don't use chicken stock and use olive oil in place of the butter). It's good with eggs, soft-boiled, fried or poached, and, to bump up your five-a-day, stir in a bag of baby spinach leaves at the end and really feel virtuous.

**Serves 4 as a main course
or 6 as a starter**

1 onion, cut in half from root to tip
    and thinly sliced into half-moons
25 g (1 oz/2 tablespoons) salted
    or unsalted butter
2 tablespoons extra-virgin olive oil
salt and freshly ground black pepper
150 g (5 oz) artichokes from a jar in oil,
    drained
200 g (7 oz) young fresh or frozen broad
    (fava) beans
200 g (7 oz) fresh or frozen peas
500 ml (17 fl oz/2¼ cups) chicken
    or vegetable stock or hot water
large handful (approximately 30 g/1 oz)
    of finely chopped green herbs such
    as wild fennel, parsley, celery leaves,
    dill, mint
2 teaspoons red or white wine vinegar
100 g (3½ oz) baby spinach (optional)

Fry the onion in the butter and half of the oil with the seasoning over a medium heat until soft. Add the rest of the ingredients (except the spinach) and bring to the boil. Turn the heat down to a simmer and continue to cook for around 15 minutes. This might seem longer than usual for young vegetables but cooking them for longer brings out the sweetness and improves the whole dish. Towards the end of cooking, stir in the spinach leaves to wilt, if using. Serve hot or at room temperature with the remaining olive oil swirled over the top.

ROMANO PEPPERS STUFFED WITH PORK MINCE & HERBS

I have always wondered what to do with the long, slim red peppers that appear in the shops in summer. We ate these delicious peppers stuffed with a meat filling as part of antipasti cooked by our friend Mimmo at Osteria Bacchus, in Sant'Ambrogio, perched on a hill just outside Cefalù. I love herbs and have included a huge handful in this recipe, but don't feel it has to be made up solely of parsley – a mixture of leaves, such as rocket (arugula), oregano, basil or celery, would do just as well.

**Serves 8 as a main course
or 16 as antipasti**

---

seed oil for frying
8 long red Romano peppers

For the stuffing
100 g (3½ oz/½ cup) wholegrain
    brown rice
1 red onion, finely chopped
salt and freshly ground black pepper
2 tablespoons extra-virgin olive oil
300 g (10½ oz/1⅓ cups) minced
    (ground) pork
finely grated zest of 1 lemon
2 eggs, beaten
50 g (2 oz) parsley, finely chopped
50 g (2 oz) Parmesan, finely grated,
    plus extra to taste (optional)

Preheat the oven to 240°C (475°F/Gas 9). Boil the rice in salted water for 25–30 minutes until soft. Rinse in a sieve under cold running water to cool, and set aside to drain. Meanwhile, fry the onion with some seasoning in the oil in a non-stick frying pan until soft – this should take around 10 minutes. Transfer the onion to a plate and allow to cool. Put all the stuffing ingredients into a bowl and mix well with your hands. Test the mixture by rolling a small patty and frying it in a pan with a little seed oil. If you are happy with the taste of the mixture go ahead and stuff the peppers, or adjust the seasoning and add more cheese and then continue.

Halve the peppers around the middle and use your fingers to pull the seeds and core out of each cavity. Stuff the insides with the mixture. Make up any leftover mixture into walnut-sized meatballs and cook alongside the peppers (these are ideal for fussy children who don't like peppers – not mentioning any names!). Place on a baking tray and roast for 12–15 minutes or until the peppers are lightly blackened and the pork is cooked through. To test this, pierce one of the peppers with a skewer and make sure the juices that run out are clear and not pink, or use a probe thermometer and check the internal temperature has reached 75°C (167°F). Allow to cool a little before serving. The peppers can be eaten as they are with a salad, with the Sicilian Chips on page 98 or a vegetable dish, or cut into rings and served as canapés.

BAKED AUBERGINE WITH TOMATO SAUCE & MOZZARELLA

Pat Frustaci's grandmother Rosina Alongi was born in Sicily and emigrated to the US in the early 1900s. She cooked every day, even when she turned 101. According to her, the true Italian dish was aubergine (eggplant) parmigiana. She liked to claim that Sicilians created the dish because of the abundance of aubergines grown in the region, but offered the possibility that it was invented in Parma, Italy, where the cheese originated. Pat's guess is that even today the two regions are probably still arguing over the ownership of this fabulous dish.

This is Giancarlo's version, which we sell in our restaurant Caffè Caldesi. We don't fry the aubergines or coat them in breadcrumbs as we find our customers prefer the lighter version (and this way the recipe is gluten-free). However, you will see variations on a theme throughout Sicily: some recipes use a batter or breadcrumbs, and others simply fry the aubergines after a light dusting in flour. There is no need to salt the long purple variety as any bitterness was bred out of them years ago.

Serves 8

---

6 aubergines (eggplants), topped and tailed and cut lengthways into 1 cm (½ in) thick, even slices
100 ml (3½ fl oz/scant ½ cup) extra-virgin olive oil for brushing
salt and freshly ground black pepper
1 quantity of Cherry Tomato Sauce (see page 144), blended until smooth
250 g (9 oz) cow's milk mozzarella, drained and cut into 5 mm (¼ in) cubes
100 g (3½ oz) Parmesan, finely grated
20 basil leaves

Preheat the oven to 220°C (425°F/Gas 7) and line a baking tray with baking parchment. Brush the aubergine slices with the olive oil and season lightly and evenly on both sides. Lay them on the baking tray and roast in the oven for 12–15 minutes or until lightly browned. Remove from the oven and turn the heat down to 180°C (350°F/Gas 4).

Pour one-quarter of the tomato sauce into an ovenproof dish measuring approximately 25 x 25 cm (10 x 10 in) and lay over one-quarter of the aubergine slices. Top with a quarter of the mozzarella, Parmesan and basil leaves. Repeat three times more, finishing with a layer of the two cheeses. Bake in the oven for 45–60 minutes.

RICOTTA WITH BASIL

This makes a really useful base of flavourful ricotta. In the morning in Sicily you can get freshly made, still-warm sheep's milk ricotta. However, this recipe makes even the supermarket variety taste as good. Top a bowl of hot pasta with spoonfuls of it, eat it on toast with the Sun-dried Tomato & Chilli Relish below or stir it into the Sausage & Wild Fennel Ragu on page 134.

Makes 125 g (4 oz), enough for 8 medium crostini or 4 bowls of pasta

Mix the ingredients together in a bowl and adjust the seasoning to taste.

100 g (3½ oz/⅓ cup) ricotta
1 generous tablespoon double (heavy) cream or whole milk
1 tablespoon extra-virgin olive oil
handful of finely chopped basil leaves
salt and freshly ground black pepper

SUN-DRIED TOMATO & CHILLI RELISH

I bought a tub of this useful paste at the market in Ortigia. The lady at the stand explained how it could be used. It makes a lovely/ relish to eat with the Ricotta with Basil recipe above and hot sourdough toast, or you can spread a layer onto a fillet of fish before grilling, spoon over roasted cauliflower florets or simply stir into pasta and top with finely grated pecorino or Parmesan cheese (see the photo on page 123). The fennel seeds and chilli give a little spice and heat to the paste.

Serves 6 for fish and 12 for crostini with Ricotta with Basil (above)

Soak the fennel seeds in hot water for 10 minutes to soften, then drain. Chop the seeds, tomatoes and chilli together on a board with a large cook's knife until you have a coarse paste. Spoon the paste into a bowl and add the oil. Taste and add a little salt if necessary. You probably won't need any as sun-dried tomatoes are salted when dried.

1 teaspoon fennel seeds
100 g (3½ oz/⅔ cup) sun-dried tomatoes, drained of oil
pinch of chilli flakes, to taste
3 tablespoons extra-virgin olive oil
fine salt (optional)

NAKED WILD CHARD PIE WITH GOAT'S CHEESE

Wild leaves such as chard, chicory, rocket (arugula) and other nutritious herbs are collected in bundles by foraging Sicilians. We might not be so lucky to find wild alternatives here in the UK, so you will be pleased to know a bag of spinach leaves freshly gathered from the local supermarket will suffice. In the right season, I find this an ideal way to use up my rather dog-eared spinach or chard from our garden glut. Alternatively, use the soft leaves from young spring greens or a mixture of them all. The recipe comes from our friend Ada, who runs the beautiful hotel Monaci delle Terre Nere on the slopes of Mount Etna. They grow their own organic vegetables on the fertile black earth. Ada loves healthy Mediterranean recipes and makes this pie without a pastry crust, which is why it's 'naked'!

Serves 4

butter for greasing
1 kg (2 lb 3 oz) chard leaves (tough stems discarded before weighing)
2 tablespoons extra-virgin olive oil
1 garlic clove, peeled and finely chopped
salt and freshly ground black pepper
2 eggs
200 g (7 oz) goat's cheese
100 g (3½ oz) grana padano, grated

Preheat the oven to 170°C (325°F/Gas 3) and butter a 24 cm (9½ in) loose-bottomed cake tin or line a flan tin with baking parchment.

Bring a large pot of water to the boil while you wash the chard. When the water is boiling, salt it generously and add the chard leaves. Blanch the chard for 5 minutes (if you are using spinach instead it might only need a minute or two), drain thoroughly and chop medium-fine. Heat the oil in a large frying pan and add the garlic. Fry for just 30 seconds, making sure the garlic doesn't burn, then add the chard. Fry for a couple of minutes, tossing frequently to coat the chard in the garlicky oil, and season to taste. Remove from the heat, transfer to a large mixing bowl and set aside.

Blend together the eggs, goat's cheese, grana padano and some seasoning. You can do this in a bowl with a fork or much more quickly in a food processor. Stir in the chard to combine.

Pour into the prepared tin and bake in the preheated oven for 25 minutes or until firm to the touch. Allow to cool for 5 minutes, then remove the pie from the tin. Eat straight away or allow to come to room temperature. The pie is lovely with a light salad, on its own with bread or served with the Cherry Tomato Sauce on page 144.

SWEET & SOUR AUBERGINES

This brightly coloured, almost jewel-like version of *caponata* was our favourite as we toured the island. This dish is all about achieving the correct balance between sweet and sour; care should be taken when adding the vinegar and sugar. Vincenzo Clemente, who owns the Cin Cin restaurant in Palermo, got the balance just right and taught us his version. At one point, he told us, *caponata* was covered with cocoa powder as a deterrent against flies. Too much and it is bitter but a little enriches the dish. He likes to serve this with octopus or swordfish but it is also good with bread, *panelle* (the Chickpea Fritters on page 28), cheese or sliced meats.

Caponata di pesce, made with tuna or swordfish, was originally a dish for the wealthy but the Sicilian poor replaced the fish with aubergines (eggplants). Salting is not necessary with the modern deep-purple variety as they are no longer bitter. Traditionally the aubergines are fried but we prefer to roast them in the oven.

Serves 8

2 large aubergines (eggplants)
sunflower oil for deep-frying or
    2 tablespoons extra-virgin olive oil
    for roasting
salt and ground white or black pepper
1 onion, cut in half from root to tip
    and thinly sliced into half-moons
1 garlic clove, peeled and lightly crushed
4 tablespoons extra-virgin olive oil
1 celery heart and leaves, roughly cut
    in 1 cm (½ in) cubes
50 g (2 oz/¼ cup) stoned green olives,
    roughly chopped
2 tablespoons capers in salt, rinsed
200 g (7 oz/1 cup) tinned whole tomatoes,
    roughly chopped
2 heaped tablespoons caster (superfine)
    sugar
3–4 tablespoons white wine vinegar

To serve
cocoa powder
toasted almonds or pine nuts
a few mint leaves

Top and tail the aubergines, removing a few strips of the skin along the length of each one as Vincenzo thinks too much skin makes the *caponata* bitter and chewy. Cut them into 2 cm (¾ in) cubes. Either deep-fry them in the sunflower oil until crisp and light brown, then drain on kitchen paper. Or, if roasting, toss the aubergines in a bowl with the 2 tablespoons of olive oil and some salt and pepper, then spread them out on a baking tray lined with baking parchment and cook in a preheated oven at 180°C (350°F/Gas 4) for around 20 minutes or until crisp at the edges and golden brown.

Sweat the onion and garlic in the 4 tablespoons of olive oil in a large frying pan with the celery, some salt and pepper and a little water over a low flame with the lid on. Check and stir frequently until the onion is soft – this will probably take 15–20 minutes.

Add the olives, capers and tomatoes to the celery in the frying pan and stir through. Turn up the heat to bring the mixture to a boil and add the sugar and 3 tablespoons of the vinegar. Stir and let the vinegar evaporate for 5 minutes. Taste and adjust the balance accordingly for sweet and sour, adding more vinegar if necessary. Remove the garlic.

Pour the celery mixture over the fried aubergines and allow the dish to come to room temperature before serving. The flavour improves further if it is refrigerated overnight and reheated the next day. However, always allow the *caponata* to come to room temperature before serving, and add a scattering of cocoa powder, toasted nuts or mint leaves as you wish.

RAW SEA BASS WITH A MINT & LEMON DRESSING

Raw fish dishes are enjoyed all over Italy as so much of the country lies on the coast. To eat fish raw it should be very fresh or previously commercially frozen at very low temperatures – this process kills any parasites, if you are concerned. We asked the chef-patron Carlo, at Apollonion restaurant in Ortigia, what was important about *pesce crudo* dishes. 'You must taste the fish and not the vinegar,' he told us; the marinade should be *leggera*, weak, so as not to dominate the subtle flavour of the fish straight from the market that morning. This recipe from Caterina Valentino at Il Palladio restaurant in Giardini Naxos features the ubiquitous *salmoriglio* dressing used for cooked fish as well as raw. Try adding little cubes of fruit such as peach, melon or strawberry give it a summery feel. The lemon juice 'cooks' thinly cut fish in minutes, turning it from translucent pinkish grey to opaque white.

Serves 6 as a starter

---

1 red onion, very finely sliced into rings
4 × 125 g (4 oz) fillets of very fresh sea bream, sea bass or haddock, pin-boned and skinned
¼–½ red chilli, according to taste, finely chopped
small handful of mint leaves, roughly chopped
salt and freshly ground black pepper
1 quantity of *Salmoriglio* dressing (see page 198)

Put the red onion slices into a bowl of cold water for around 15 minutes to reduce their strength of flavour. Slice the fish with a sharp knife at a 45 degree angle across the fillet so that you end up with pieces about 3 mm (⅛ in) thick. Lay the slices onto serving plates. Drain the onions and briefly dry on kitchen paper. Scatter the onions, chilli and mint over the fish. At this point, the plates can be stored in the fridge.

When ready to serve, season the fish evenly and pour over the dressing. Leave it for around 5 minutes at room temperature. The longer you leave the dressing on the fish, the more it will be 'cooked' by the acidity, so serve straight away or leave a little longer for a more 'cooked' texture.

BAKED CHEESE WITH ANCHOVIES & LEMON ZEST

On a cold evening in Palermo, we huddled into the welcoming Osteria Dei Vespri and warmed ourselves up with glasses of Nero d'Avola red wine and an antipasto of hot melting cheese in a terracotta dish with the local sesame focaccia (see page 37). They had used *tuma*, a firm mature sheep's cheese that melts when heated but holds its shape. The cheese is cut in half and filled with the sauce like a sandwich – if you can find the cheese, do try it this way. However, as *tuma* is hard to get in most shops we have adapted this very easy recipe to use the more widely available halloumi instead.

Serves 4

2 anchovy fillets in oil, drained
1 teaspoon dried oregano
finely grated zest of ½ lemon
1 tablespoon extra-virgin olive oil
225 g (8 oz) halloumi cheese

Heat a non-stick pan over a high heat. Mash the anchovies, oregano and zest with a fork in a small bowl with the oil until you have a paste. Cut the cheese into 1 cm (½ in) slices. Dry-fry the slices in the hot pan until lightly blackened on one side. Turn the slices over and brush on a thin layer of the anchovy paste while the slices are still in the pan. When the underside is just blackened, remove from the pan and serve straight away with fresh crusty bread and, if you have some, the Roast Peppers Palermo Style on page 96.

SOUPS

SOUPS

A bowl of velvety soup warms and fills you up and is like a big cuddle. Soups made from grains, legumes, vegetables and wild greens have been on the staple peasant menu for centuries when there was little else available. It was probably a very healthy way to eat even if it did leave them yearning for meat and fish. Beans have always been referred to as poor man's meat, because they are a rich source of protein. Now pasta is such a big part of the Mediterranean diet, there is a choice of soup or pasta as *primi piatti*, first course.

Broad Bean & Fennel Seed Soup

Use 3 Ways

As a vegetable, soup, sliced & fried

Dried broad (fava) beans have a distinctive, earthy flavour and a velvety texture unlike their former fresh selves. Do try them, I think the taste is perfectly lovely. In the south of Italy you can find a broad been purée probably introduced by the Romans, cooked from dried like this and served with the wilted green vegetable *cicoria*, another wonderful combination and easily reproduced with spinach.

In Sicily, you will see the word *maccu* on menus all over the island; it comes from the word *macare*, to squash. Broad beans have been a staple of the peasant diet for centuries since they can be eaten fresh and raw in spring with young soft cheeses, boiled briefly through summer and dried for use in autumn and winter. In this case, dried broad beans are soaked overnight, then boiled and squashed to make a mash. If you use split broad beans they will have already been peeled and will take less time to cook. Leave it rough and ready like the ancient peasant soup that it was, or purée it for a sophisticated starter like our friend Marco Piraino, who showed me this recipe. He garnishes it with chopped samphire, drops of good olive oil and a little lemon zest.

To make it more filling (it's already pretty substantial!), put toasted bread drizzled with olive oil into soup bowls and ladle the soup on top, or leave the soup a little rough and mix in some just-cooked short pasta. The *maccu* sets firm when cold and can be cut into slices, breaded and fried.

Serves 6

500 g (1 lb 2 oz/2 cups) dried broad
   (fava) beans, with or without skins
1 white onion, cut in half
2 teaspoons fennel seeds, roughly
   crushed in a pestle and mortar
1 celery stalk, finely sliced
2 tablespoons extra-virgin olive oil
1.6 litres (54 fl oz/6¾ cups) water
4 tablespoons white wine
salt, to taste

To serve
2 tablespoons extra-virgin olive oil
a little chopped samphire or finely
   grated lemon zest
freshly ground black pepper

Cover the beans in cold water and soak overnight. The following day, drain the beans and discard the water. Slip the beans from their skins if not already peeled.

Put all the ingredients together in a medium saucepan and bring to the boil. Turn the heat to low and let the beans bubble away until they are tender and easily squashed, up to 2 hours, adding a little more water if necessary. Keep a couple of tablespoons of the whole beans to one side for garnish. Purée the soup as much or as little as you like with a stick blender. Pour into warm bowls and garnish with the reserved beans, a swirl of olive oil and the lemon zest or chopped samphire. Finish with a twist of black pepper.

Variations:
As a vegetable side dish
As the beans are cooking, don't add extra water but let the mixture become thick. Purée the mixture to a rough or smooth texture and use it as you would mashed potato. In the south of Italy you will often see this served with garlicky sautéed spinach or chard leaves on top.

For sliced *maccu*
After blending the soup pour it into a lined loaf tin and allow to cool. Put it into the fridge overnight and it will set firm. It can then be cut into 1.5 cm (½ in) slices and dipped in flour, egg and breadcrumbs (like the Chicken Parmigiana on page 180) and fried in hot oil until browned. Drain it on kitchen paper and serve straight away, dusted in a little salt.

Above: Broad Bean & Fennel Seed Soup. Below: Chickpea & Apple Soup.

CHICKPEA & APPLE SOUP

This unusual sweet-tasting and textural soup is from our chef friend Marco Piraino from Palermo. It makes a gorgeous first course or lunchtime meal. Chickpeas are a very good source of protein, fibre and minerals and have formed an important part of the Italian diet for centuries (see photo on page 77).

Serves 6

250 g (9 oz/1¼ cups) dried chickpeas
3 tablespoons extra-virgin olive oil,
    plus extra to serve
1 leek, trimmed and finely chopped
2 apples, peeled and roughly chopped
1 bay leaf
1 garlic clove, peeled, cored and crushed
3 litres (102 fl oz/12¾ cups) water
    or chicken or vegetable stock
salt and freshly ground black pepper

Cover the chickpeas in cold water and soak overnight. The following day drain them and discard the water. Heat the oil in a large saucepan and fry the leek for 5 minutes over a medium heat until softened, then add the rest of the ingredients and stir through. Cook until the chickpeas are soft, which should take around 1½ hours but could be up to 2½ hours depending on how old they are. Add a little more hot water if it starts to dry out. You can blend the soup as much or as little as you like with a stick blender in the saucepan. Check the seasoning and adjust as necessary. Pour the soup into warm bowls and finish with a swirl of good olive oil and a twist of black pepper.

TOMATO & RICE SOUP

Originally all rice was brown, before mills were designed to remove the husk and polish the grains. It is much better for you as it is the whole grain and I much prefer the taste of brown rice. This is real peasant soup; add what vegetables are in season or what you have at the back of the fridge. The soup is fabulous on its own but with the topping it's sublime. The breadcrumbs were a way of mimicking grated cheese on a dish when poverty made this unaffordable. I was really impressed by the use of the Sicilian *estrattu*, a seriously concentrated salty tomato purée, on our visits there. It is an ingredient like Worcestershire sauce in the UK or soy sauce in Asia – it just makes everything taste better. We have replaced it with tomato purée (tomato paste) but if you are on a trip to Sicily do grab some; it is so rich and deep in wonderful umami flavour. As it is salty, don't add any salt to the cooking if you are using it.

Serves 6–8

---

1 large onion, roughly chopped
3 celery stalks, roughly chopped
3 small carrots, roughly chopped
2 tablespoons extra-virgin olive oil
2 tablespoons chicken fat or
    2 tablespoons more of olive oil
salt and freshly ground black pepper
½ teaspoon chilli flakes (optional)
2 tablespoons *estrattu* or tomato purée
    (tomato paste)
2 litres (68 fl oz/8½ cups) warm chicken
    or vegetable stock
150 g (5 oz/¾ cup) brown rice
1 x 400 g tin whole plum tomatoes
2 bay leaves
1 piece of Parmesan rind (optional)
100 g (3½ oz) baby spinach leaves

For the breadcrumb topping
1 small handful of parsley
1 slice gluten-free or wheat bread
1 small garlic clove, peeled
salt and freshly ground black pepper
35 g (1¼ oz) Parmesan, finely grated
2 tablespoons extra-virgin olive oil

Fry the onion, celery and carrots in the oil and chicken fat (if using) in a large saucepan over a medium heat until they start to soften. Season well with salt and pepper and the chilli flakes, if using. In a small bowl soften the *estrattu* with a little of the warm stock. Add to the pan with the remaining stock, the rice, tomatoes, bay leaves and rind of Parmesan, if using. Use a potato masher to break up the tomatoes to a pulp. Leave to cook for around 25 minutes or until the rice is cooked and softened.

Meanwhile, make the breadcrumbs for the topping. Preheat the oven to 180°C (350°F/Gas 4). Whizz the parsley with the bread, garlic and some seasoning in a food processor to make fine breadcrumbs. Pour them into a bowl and stir through the Parmesan and olive oil. Spread onto a baking tray and cook in the oven for 5–7 minutes or until the breadcrumbs become crunchy. Remove from the oven and tip onto a plate to cool.

When the rice is cooked, stir in the spinach leaves – they will wilt easily in the heat. Serve the soup in warmed bowls topped with the breadcrumbs.

A SOUP OF TWO HALVES

This soup is a bright green bowlful of health and flavour. It's perfect for using up any greens lurking in your fridge, or if you have a glut of leafy veg. Use both the white and soft green parts of the spring onions or leeks to make the base. My inspiration came from the *tenerumi* soup so enjoyed in late summer and made with the leaves of the long green courgettes (zucchini). To serve, we like to grate feta cheese on top in place of salted ricotta, add a pile of (bell) peppers and then scatter over herbs in two halves so that you can have a mouthful of soup with wild fennel or dill or one with mint. It makes a great talking point at the table as people debate which one they prefer.

Serves 6–8

2 red or yellow (bell) peppers
1 bunch of spring onions (15–20 g/
 ½–¾ oz) or 2 leeks, trimmed and
 roughly chopped
1 celery heart with leaves, roughly
 chopped (25 g/1 oz)
3 garlic cloves, peeled
4 tablespoons extra-virgin olive oil
500 g (1 lb 2 oz) assorted leaves such
 as spinach, carrot tops, baby kale,
 chard, parsley, rocket (arugula),
 watercress, lettuce (or peas)
25 g (1 oz) parsley leaves and stalks,
 roughly chopped
25 g (1 oz/1 cup) basil leaves
1 litre (34 fl oz/4¼ cups) stock, such
 as vegetable or light chicken, or water
salt and freshly ground black pepper

To serve
200 g (7 oz/¾ cup) salted ricotta or feta
handful of two different herbs, such
 as dill or wild fennel, mint or basil
 or coriander (cilantro) or chervil or
 sweet cicely
extra-virgin olive oil

Preheat the oven to 220°C (425°F/Gas 7). Place the peppers on a baking tray and cook in the oven to blacken them – this should take around 20 minutes. Transfer them to a bowl and cover with cling film (plastic wrap) to sweat and cool. Meanwhile, fry the onions or leeks, celery and garlic in the oil in a large saucepan over a gentle heat for around 10 minutes or until the vegetables have begun to soften.

Add the leaves and herbs and stir through. Pour in the stock and bring to the boil. Reduce the heat to a simmer and allow the leaves to soften for around 5 minutes.

At this point, peel the peppers under cold running water, deseed, roughly chop and set aside. Remove the soup from the heat and blend using a stick blender. If you use a blender or food processor, blend in batches so that hot soup doesn't leak out. Check the seasoning and serve straight away, or allow to cool and store in the fridge until you need it. It will keep for 3 days in the fridge.

Serve the soup in wide bowls with ricotta or feta grated over and a pile of the roasted peppers on top. Sprinkle the herbs in two different areas, give a final twist of black pepper and a swirl of good extra-virgin olive oil and serve. Ask your guests to guess the flavour. They will probably say different things depending on where they start eating!

MEATBALLS IN BROTH

We saw these tiny meatballs ready-made and for sale in a butcher's shop in Scicli. The butcher explained they were for a soup. I thought it sounded delicious. Also in Scicli is La Grotta, a cave-dwelling restaurant, where we ate this fabulous soup and begged the owner Angelo for his recipe. This is a meal in its own right, particularly if you serve it with hunks of crusty bread or add 75 g (2½ oz) rice or tiny pasta shapes such as *stelline*, 'little stars', to the stock. You can add vegetables if you like, and you can stir in spinach leaves or shredded kale at the end for a green finale.

> **Serves 4 (makes 25–30 balls around 3 cm/1¼ in wide)**

For the stock
1 carrot, roughly chopped
1 celery stalk and leaves from the heart, roughly chopped
1 onion, roughly chopped
1 bay leaf
1 sprig of rosemary
cooked chicken carcass or meat bones (optional)
3 tablespoons extra-virgin olive oil
2 litres (68 fl oz/8½ cups) hot water

For the meatballs
250 g (9 oz/1 cup) minced (ground) beef or pork, or a mixture of the two or cooked meat or stuffing
30 g (1 oz) Parmesan, finely grated
30 g (1 oz/scant ¼ cup) fresh breadcrumbs, made from gluten-free or wheat bread
1 shallot, very finely chopped or grated
1 teaspoon salt
freshly ground black pepper, to taste
1 heaped tablespoon finely chopped parsley
1–2 eggs
3 tablespoons extra-virgin olive oil for frying

For the green breadcrumbs
100 g (3½ oz) stale gluten-free or wheat bread, crusts removed
small handful of parsley
1 tablespoon chopped celery leaves (optional)
½ tablespoon rosemary needles
1 small garlic clove, peeled

25 g (1 oz) grated Parmesan, to serve

First make the stock by frying the vegetables with the herbs, and the bones if you have them, in the oil until lightly browned and just starting to stick on the bottom of the saucepan. Pour in the water and bring to the boil. Turn the heat down to medium and let the stock simmer gently while you make the meatballs. Remove the rosemary after 20 minutes.

Combine the ingredients for the meatballs in a bowl with your hands. If you are using cooked meat or stuffing, you may need a second egg to bind the mixture together. Make one small meatball and flatten slightly. Fry it in a frying pan with a little of the oil and taste to make sure you are happy with the seasoning. If not, adjust the mixture accordingly. Then make up the rest of the meatballs – they should be just smaller than a walnut as they swell in the broth when cooking. Remove the bones, if using, from the broth with a pair of tongs and discard.

Fry the meatballs briefly in the remaining oil until browned all over then lift out with a slotted spoon and add to the stock. Cook for 15–20 minutes until the meatballs are cooked through. Taste the broth and adjust the seasoning as necessary.

To make the breadcrumbs, whizz the ingredients together in a food processor until they have a coarse, sandy texture. Season to taste and whizz again. The breadcrumbs can be mixed with a couple of tablespoons of olive oil and fried or oven baked for a crunchy texture or left soft.

Serve the soup in warm bowls with the green breadcrumbs and Parmesan on the side, ready to sprinkle over.

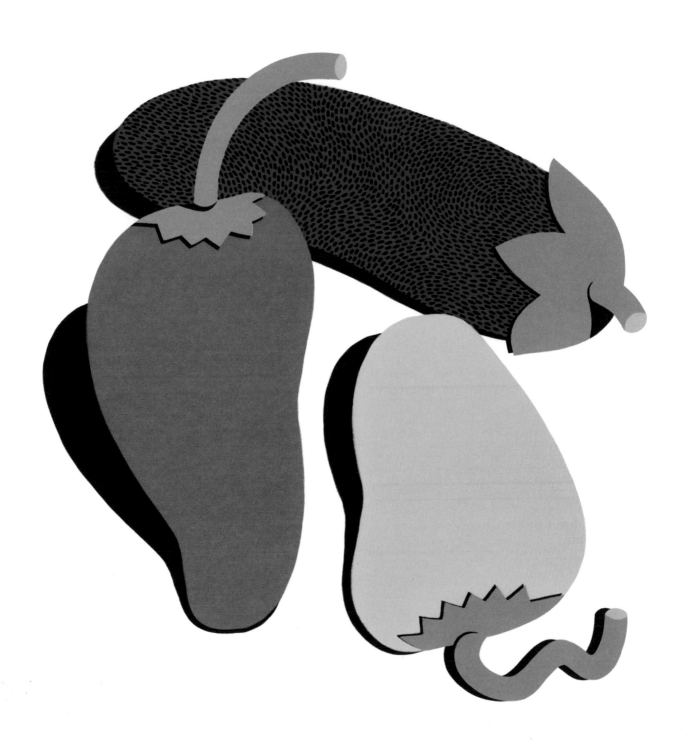

CONTORNI

CONTORNI

Any well-travelled vegetarian will tell you Sicily offers no problems for the plant-based eater. So many interesting dishes are constructed purely from vegetables.

As necessity is the mother of invention, the poor, during Sicily's centuries of poverty, would use vegetables to imitate the dishes of the rich: aubergines (eggplants) were thinly sliced to emulate veal escalopes or fillets of fish, and pumpkin used instead of liver. Freely gathered herbs such as wild fennel are used abundantly in the Sicilian kitchen. The seeds from its yellow blooms are dried to use in winter, along with tiny oregano leaves and their intricate flowers. Wild leaves like chard, rocket (arugula) and chicory have traditionally been gathered by foragers and you can still see people doing this for their own purposes or to sell at a market.

Angelo, the chef-patron at La Grotta restaurant in Scicli, told us that the local shepherds would be away for a week at a time looking after their sheep. They would take a satchel of bread (after a week you could still eat it), onions and cheese, and perhaps supplement these with local wild leaves and herbs along the way. How simple and most likely wonderful to eat.

Having written our book *Around the World in Salads* you might say I have become a bit obsessed with salad. There are times when I just yearn for raw, fresh, crisp leaves and lots of vegetables. Since Giancarlo and our son Giorgio can no longer have gluten in their diets, eating more vegetables has changed the way we live and eat.

COURGETTE RIBBONS IN LEMON & OREGANO DRESSING

Salmoriglio is used all over Sicily, mainly for dressing fish, and each cook has their own special way of making it. We loved this version made by Caterina at the Palladio hotel in Giardini Naxos; she uses it on courgettes (zucchini) thinly sliced into almost transparent ribbons, but you could spiralise them if you have the gadget. This sauce has revolutionised the way we eat vegetables – you can use it over steamed cauliflower, carrot ribbons, mangetout (snow peas) or sugar snap peas. The salting and sauce allow the vegetables to keep well in the fridge for a couple of days and they make a really healthy and delicious snack when you are feeling peckish. The *salmoriglio* sauce will keep for up to four days.

Serves 4–6

500 g (1 lb 2 oz) courgettes (zucchini)
  (around 4 medium)
1 teaspoon salt
juice of 1 lemon
freshly ground black pepper, to serve

For the dressing
large handful (approximately 15 g/½ oz)
  of parsley
1 small garlic clove, peeled
1 heaped teaspoon dried or fresh
  oregano
4 tablespoons extra-virgin olive oil

Wash the courgettes and trim away the tops and tails. Use a potato peeler to slice them into ribbons. I usually do this until it becomes hard to hold them, then I lay the courgettes on a board and continue to scrape away without the fear of injury. Put the ribbons into a bowl with the salt and lemon juice. Toss with your hands to combine and set aside for 30 minutes.

Meanwhile, make the dressing. Finely chop the parsley and garlic together on a board with a large cook's knife and put into a bowl. Pour over 3 tablespoons of boiling water and add the oregano. Use the back of a spoon to press the herbs and garlic down in the water – this helps to release the essential oils and adds to the flavour. Pour in the oil and set aside to cool.

Take the courgettes from their bowl and give them a gentle squeeze in your fist to rid them of excess water. Put them into a large mixing bowl. Pour over the dressing and, using tongs, toss to combine. Serve straight away on a platter and sprinkle over a little freshly crushed black pepper.

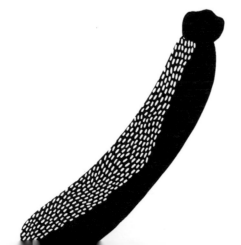

CAULIFLOWER IN RED WINE

This unusual combination of flavours adds up to much more than the sum of its parts. The recipe was given to me by Gino Borella, an Italian chef of great standing who worked for a while with a Sicilian chef who taught him this in his youth. I suspect it is one of those Sicilian dishes that was developed by the poor: having only vegetables to work with, this is what they came up with instead of meat in red wine sauce, and jolly delicious it is, too.

Try it with roast meat, or enjoy it on its own like a chunky soup in a bowl or mixed with cannellini beans or on top of brown rice. I've also served it as part of a spread of antipasti. Always serve it warm with bread to mop up the wonderfully umami juices.

Serves 4–6

---

5 anchovy fillets in oil, drained
4 garlic cloves, peeled
4 tablespoons extra-virgin olive oil
600–700 g (1 lb 5 oz–1 lb 8 oz) cauliflower, broken into walnut-sized florets
250 ml (8½ fl oz/1 cup) red wine
1 tablespoon tomato purée (tomato paste)
100 ml (3½ fl oz/scant ½ cup) vegetable stock or water
salt (optional) and freshly ground black pepper
50 g (2 oz/½ stick) salted butter
small bunch of parsley, chopped

Finely chop the anchovies and garlic together on a board. Heat the oil in a large frying pan and fry the anchovy mixture over a low heat for a few minutes until the anchovies dissolve. Do keep the heat low so as not to burn the garlic.

Meanwhile, parboil the cauliflower for 3 minutes in boiling salted water. Drain and add to the frying pan. Keep tossing the cauliflower so that the florets are well covered with the anchovy mixture and cook for about 5 minutes, taking care not to let it burn, then add the wine and bring to the boil.

Add the tomato purée, stock and black pepper. Boil again for a couple of minutes, then stir in the butter and, when melted, reduce the temperature to a slow simmer for 10–15 minutes until the cauliflower is cooked through. Check the seasoning and add more pepper and some salt if necessary. Stir in the parsley and serve.

SWEET & SOUR AUBERGINES WITH TOASTED ALMONDS

This richly coloured and flavoured vegetable dish goes perfectly with fried or grilled (broiled) meats. It is similar to *Caponata* (see page 65) but rather quicker to make. Traditionally, the aubergines (eggplants) are fried but we have roasted them for a healthier twist (see page 182 for photo).

Serves 4–6

2 aubergines (eggplants)
5 tablespoons extra-virgin olive oil
salt and freshly ground black pepper
50 g (2 oz) blanched, unblanched
  or flaked almonds
1 shallot, finely chopped
3 tablespoons tomato purée
  (tomato paste)
150 ml (5 fl oz/⅔ cup) water
2 tablespoons white or red wine vinegar
3 tablespoons caster (superfine) sugar
small handful of mint leaves, to serve

Preheat the oven to 200°C (400°F/Gas 6) and line a baking tray with baking parchment. Top and tail the aubergines, cut into finger-size sticks and place in a large bowl. Drizzle over 2 tablespoons of the oil and toss to coat with a little seasoning. Lay the aubergine sticks on the baking tray and roast in the oven for 15–20 minutes until browned at the edges and soft. Toast the almonds in a dry frying pan (skillet) or a hot oven for up to 10 minutes or until golden brown and set aside to cool before roughly chopping.

Meanwhile, fry the shallot in the remaining oil in a frying pan until soft and then add the tomato purée, water, vinegar, sugar and some salt. Bring to the boil and then turn down the heat to low and simmer, uncovered, for around 20 minutes. It is really important to adjust the balance of sweet and sour to your taste as well as the amount of salt. Remove the sauce from the heat and add the aubergines, stir through and serve straight away or allow to cool to room temperature. Scatter over the almonds and mint leaves before serving.

ROAST PEPPERS PALERMO STYLE

These colourful sweet (bell) peppers are excellent as a side dish to accompany eggs, baked fish and grilled (broiled) meats or as part of a spread of antipasti. Marco Piraino, our chef friend from Palermo, showed me this local way of cooking them. Sicilians use a lot of dry, fine breadcrumbs as they were meant to imitate grated Parmesan by the poor. Any breadcrumbs will work for this recipe. In fact, larger breadcrumbs from a fresh sourdough loaf make a wonderfully crunchy topping instead of fine.

Serves 6–8

2 red and 2 yellow (bell) peppers,
    seeded and cut into thin strips
1 onion, cut in half from root to tip
    and thinly sliced into half-moons
6 tablespoons extra-virgin olive oil
salt and freshly ground black pepper
4 tablespoons pine nuts
4 tablespoons raisins
30 g (1 oz) Pecorino Siciliano or
    Parmesan, finely grated
30 g (1 oz/scant ⅓ cup) fine dry
    breadcrumbs (can be gluten-free)
1 tablespoon dried oregano

Preheat the oven to 170°C (325°F/Gas 3) and line a baking tray with baking parchment. Mix the peppers, onion, oil, some seasoning, pine nuts and raisins together in a bowl to combine. Pour the mixture onto the baking tray and cook in the oven for 40–45 minutes or until it is slightly crisp.

Meanwhile, stir the cheese, breadcrumbs and oregano together and 5 minutes before the end of the cooking time remove the tray from the oven and scatter over the peppers. Give a rough stir through and put back into the oven to brown. When the peppers are slightly browned on the edges and soft the dish is ready to serve, either piping hot or cooled to room temperature.

SICILIAN CHIPS

Inspired by our recent trips in search of Sicilian flavours, I found myself adding oregano to almost everything. We love these potatoes cooked in this way and enjoy them with fish or meat – our son Flavio would eat the lot just as they are! Oregano is sold in bunches in Sicilian markets, so do bring some back with you if you are visiting. Keep it in the bag and simply roll it between your hands to release the tiny dried leaves. Olives bought with the stone in always taste better; just squash them with the flat of a large knife to release the stone. If you can't find Italian olives, Kalamata olives from Greece are just as good. If you are going for a more sophisticated look, cut the potatoes into discs around 5 mm (¼ in) thick instead of chips.

Serves 4–6

---

1 kg (2 lb 3 oz) potatoes, peeled and cut into chips
1 onion, cut from root to tip and sliced into half-moons the same width as the chips
7 tablespoons extra-virgin olive oil
2 teaspoons dried oregano
salt and freshly ground black pepper
150 g (5 oz) cherry tomatoes, cut in half
handful of good-quality black olives, stoned and split open (optional)

Preheat the oven to 200°C (400°F/Gas 6) and line a baking tray with baking parchment. Toss the ingredients together in a bowl and spread them out evenly on the baking tray. Bake for 30–35 minutes or until golden brown and cooked through. Remove from the oven and transfer to a warm serving dish. Serve hot.

SWEET & SOUR PUMPKIN

Like many Sicilian dishes that use vegetables instead of meat, this recipe is an adaptation by the poor man of the wealthy man's food. Pumpkin was supposed to be the vegetable equivalent of liver, in a sweet and sour sauce. Do use pumpkin or butternut squash for the recipe. I like to leave the skins on if using squash. Sometimes, though, I do cheat and buy the bags of ready-cut slices of squash, in which case they may take less time to cook. This is good with fish or meat dishes, or as part of a spread of antipasti.

Serves 6

---

600 g (1 lb 5 oz) pumpkin or butternut
    squash, sliced into 1 cm (½ in)
    thick wedges
5 tablespoons extra-virgin olive oil
salt and freshly ground black pepper
2 garlic cloves, peeled and roughly sliced
small handful of mint leaves
1 tablespoon caster (superfine) sugar
2 tablespoons white wine vinegar

Preheat the oven to 200°C (400°F/Gas 6). In a bowl toss the pumpkin in 3 tablespoons of the oil and add some seasoning. Lay the wedges on a baking tray in a single layer and roast in the oven for up to 30–35 minutes or until they are lightly browned and soft all the way through. Remove from the oven and use tongs to transfer the pumpkin to a shallow serving dish.

Pour any leftover oil from the tray into a frying pan and add the remaining oil. Add the garlic to the pan and fry gently over a medium heat for a few minutes. Add most of the mint to the pan, keeping aside a little for garnish. Pour in the caster sugar and vinegar and allow them to bubble for a couple of minutes. Taste the sauce to check the balance of sweet and sour, and adjust accordingly. Pour over the pumpkin wedges and allow the dish to sit at room temperature for at least 1 hour before serving. The pumpkin will keep in the fridge for around 3 days but do bring it to room temperature before serving, scattered with the remaining mint.

PURPLE SPROUTING BROCCOLI WITH SPICY ALMOND CRUNCH

Sicilians love their cruciferous vegetables and throughout the year there will always be one available such as broccoli, cauliflower or Romanesco. This crunchy topping will work with any of these. My favourite is purple sprouting broccoli as it is full of flavour, cooks quickly and makes its welcome first appearance in late winter/early spring while most other young greens are still fast asleep.

Serves 6–8

400 g (14 oz) purple sprouting broccoli
3 tablespoons extra-virgin olive oil
salt and freshly ground black pepper

For the topping
25 g (1 oz/¼ cup) flaked almonds
1 garlic clove, peeled and finely chopped
finely grated zest of ¼ lemon
pinch of chilli flakes or chopped
    fresh chilli

First make the topping by toasting the almonds in a hot oven (preheated to around 200°C/400°F/Gas 6) for 5 minutes or in a dry pan until lightly browned. Remove from the heat and leave to cool. Blitz briefly in a food processor or roughly chop by hand. Transfer to a bowl and combine with the garlic, lemon zest and chilli.

Trim any very tough stems from the ends of the broccoli florets and cut any large ones in half lengthways. Steam or boil the florets for 3–4 minutes until just tender. Drain and transfer to a warm serving dish. Toss with the oil, salt and pepper to taste and then with the spicy almonds. Serve straight away.

CITRUS COUSCOUS SALAD FROM MANDRANOVA

This recipe is based on one from Silvia Di Vincenzo from the beautiful *agriturismo* Mandranova on an olive tree estate near Agrigento. We went to stay there during one of our tours of the island and it happened to be just after the olives were pressed. At Mandranova, the oil is everything and rightly so. When we were there, Silvia's husband Giuseppe had just produced the new oil of the year – it was bright green and fruity with a full-bodied intensity and the flavour of newly-mown grass and tomatoes, thanks to the large green Nocellara olives used to make it. Silvia loves to use her homemade oil in her cooking, and each one imparts a different flavour to the dish.

Serves 6–8

5 spring onions, roughly chopped
    into 1 cm (½ in) lengths
150 g (5 oz/generous ⅔ cup) wheat
    or maize couscous
50 g (2 oz/½ cup) flaked almonds
50 g (2 oz/½ cup) pine nuts
50 g (2 oz/⅓ cup) stoned green olives,
    roughly chopped
150 g (5 oz) leaves, such as basil, parsley,
    rocket (arugula), celery and coriander
    (cilantro), roughly chopped

For the dressing
5 tablespoons fruity extra-virgin olive oil
juice of 1 lemon
juice of 1 orange
1 teaspoon runny honey
salt and freshly ground black pepper

Preheat the oven 200°C/400°F/Gas 6.

Soak the spring onions in cold water for 15 minutes to reduce the strength. Soak the couscous in hot water or stock according to the packet instructions. Put the nuts on a baking tray and brown in the oven for 5–7 minutes. When golden tip onto a plate to cool.

To make the dressing, stir the ingredients together in a small bowl, seasoning to taste.

Fluff up the couscous with a fork, fold in the remaining ingredients and the dressing. Adjust the seasoning as necessary and serve at room temperature.

LEMON & ORANGE SALAD

The shell-shaped area of Palermo is called the Conca d'Oro, which means 'golden shell'. It is where the Arabs started growing lemon trees. It is said that the Mafia took root here, when the locals were paid protection money by wealthy absentee landlords to look after the lemon trees.

This salad, based on the plentiful citrus fruit that still grows in Sicily, was discovered by our agent and friend Sheila Abelman on a walking trip around Sicily. I am very grateful to her; she took notes and photos to show me after her trip so that I could recreate the dish here. It is refreshing all year around and best left at room temperature for an hour to two before serving, to let the flavours meld together.

Serves 4–6

1 large red or white onion or 5 spring
   onions, cut into very small dice
4 oranges
1 large lemon
3 tablespoons extra-virgin olive oil
3 tablespoons white wine
small handful of finely chopped parsley
   leaves and thin stalks
salt and freshly ground black pepper

Soak the onion in cold water for 15 minutes – this will dispel the strong flavour. Meanwhile, prepare the rest of the salad. On a board and using a sharp knife, peel and cut away the pith from the oranges. Cut out the segments from between the membrane and let them fall on to a large serving dish. Do the same with the lemon but cut the segments into four and scatter them over the oranges. Pour over the oil and white wine and evenly scatter over the parsley and season to taste.

MELON, ORANGE & WALNUT SALAD

This is a really quick salad to throw together and enjoy as a starter or after a main course. Almost any melon will work for this recipe, depending on the season. Do pick one that is ripe and has plenty of flavour. You can usually tell this by smelling the top of it. If there is no scent, choose another one or wait until it ripens. You need a really good, peppery olive oil for this – the flavour with the orange and melon is worth the expense.

Serves 6

---

1 melon (approximately 1–1.5 kg/2 lb 3 oz–3 lb 5 oz), peeled, seeded and cut into 2 cm (¾ in) thick wedges
2 oranges
2 tablespoons small and torn large mint leaves
3 tablespoons extra-virgin olive oil
handful of walnuts, roughly crushed in a pestle and mortar
1 teaspoon finely grated orange zest
finely grated zest of ½ lemon
salt, to taste
2 teaspoons pink peppercorns, roughly crushed

Assemble the melon pieces on a large platter or individual plates. On a board and using a sharp knife, peel and cut away the pith from both oranges. Cut out the segments from between the membrane and let them fall on to the melon. Scatter over the remaining ingredients.

ANCHOVY, BEAN, CELERY & CAPER SALAD

On the winding road to Scicli, olive trees shelter pretty white flowers, and capers cling to the dry-stone walls dividing the terrain. Scicli is a baroque beauty, a cluster of churches, a piazza or two, potted palms and golden-yellow stone buildings that reflect the sunshine. On our way through the town, we called in for lunch at La Grotta, its name a nod to its unusual setting, nestled into the side of a cave. The restaurant is run by Angelo Di Tommasi and his son and we loved the food, especially the starter of anchovies, fronds of wild fennel (or dill), celery and *fagioli cosaruciaru*, a slow-food bean that, when cooked, melts in your mouth. We immediately popped back into the town and bought some. For ease, we have substituted them with cannellini beans in this recipe. Serve this dish with fish in *Salmoriglio* (see page 198), on its own, with chopped boiled eggs or roasted peppers, tuna or on bruschetta.

Serves 6–8

250 g (9 oz/1¼ cups) dried cannellini beans
a few sage leaves
2 garlic cloves, peeled
1 teaspoon bicarbonate of soda (baking soda) (if needed)
7 tablespoons extra-virgin olive oil
1 red onion, finely sliced
2 celery stalks and leaves from the heart, finely sliced
2 tablespoons capers in salt, rinsed
50 g (2 oz/¼ cup) good-quality black olives, stoned and chopped
2 tablespoons red wine vinegar
salt and freshly ground black pepper
handful of parsley leaves and soft stalks, finely chopped
8–10 anchovies in oil, drained, added according to taste and size, roughly chopped

Cover the beans in cold water and soak overnight. The following day, drain the beans, discard the water and put the beans into a large saucepan with twice the volume of cold water, the sage leaves and garlic. Bring to the boil and then reduce to a simmer and cook for 2–2½ hours or until soft. Top up with hot water as necessary. If the skins remain tough after this time add a teaspoon of bicarbonate of soda and cook for 5 minutes more. Drain and throw away the water. Discard the sage leaves and garlic. Put the beans into a large bowl and set aside.

Add 2 tablespoons of the oil to a frying pan and fry the onion with the celery stalks but not the leaves over a low heat for around 10 minutes or until the onion has softened. Stir through the capers and olives to coat in the cooking juices and cook for a couple of minutes. Remove from the heat and add to the beans, stirring to mix.

Make a dressing by combining the vinegar, the remaining oil and some seasoning. Mix with the beans and leave to cool. When the beans are at room temperature, stir through the parsley, celery leaves and anchovies. Taste and adjust the seasoning as necessary and maybe add a couple more anchovies if you like their flavour. Serve straight away.

Variations: Add a tin of sustainably caught tuna or some roasted red or yellow (bell) peppers.

ORANGE & FENNEL SALAD

This traditional Sicilian salad of fennel and orange is served all over the island. I like to add chicken as I think it makes a wonderful, light salad for lunch or on a hot summer's night. Alternatively, serve the salad with grilled fish. Pick a strong-flavoured, fruity extra-virgin olive oil for this salad – it makes all the difference. Try to find Sicilian oranges, if you can, for their natural sweetness or choose blood oranges when in season. See the photo on page 112.

Serves 4

3 oranges
2 white fennel bulbs, woody ends and tough outer leaves removed, finely sliced
4 tablespoons extra-virgin olive oil
small handful of pistachios, roughly chopped
small handful of wild fennel or dill sprigs
salt and freshly ground black pepper
handful of pitted green olives, roughly chopped (optional)
½ green chilli, finely chopped (optional)

Peel 2 of the oranges and cut out the segments. Do this over a bowl to catch the juices. Cut the remaining orange into very thin slices. Put all the ingredients into the bowl and season to taste. Arrange on a serving platter and decorate with the orange slices.

Variation: Add 400 g (14 oz) cooked chicken, torn into shreds, for a main course salad.

BROAD BEAN SALAD WITH LEMON & FETA

Sicilians are crazy for their broad (fava) beans, eaten either fresh and raw straight from the pod with young white cheese, or boiled and stirred into a casserole like the *Frittedda* on page 52 or dried and made into a soup (see page 76). In this recipe we have taken the idea of the young beans – still tender so you don't need to slip off the skins – and combined them with the fresh flavours of spring for a salad. This is lovely with other salads or with barbecued meats and chicken.

Serves 4–6

400 g (14 oz) frozen or young fresh broad (fava) beans
3 tablespoons extra-virgin olive oil
3 tablespoons roughly torn mint leaves
50 g (2 oz/¼ cup) salted ricotta or feta, coarsely grated
25 g (1 oz/¼ cup) toasted flaked almonds,
    roughly chopped
finely grated zest of ½ lemon
salt and freshly ground black pepper

Cook the beans for 4–5 minutes in boiling salted water. Drain and rinse under cold running water to cool quickly. Pour into a bowl and add the rest of the ingredients, seasoning to taste. Serve straight away, or up to a day later, at room temperature. The flavours meld together after around 30 minutes.

Variation: Older, larger beans can be used but boil them for up to 7 minutes until tender and squeeze them out of their tough skins.

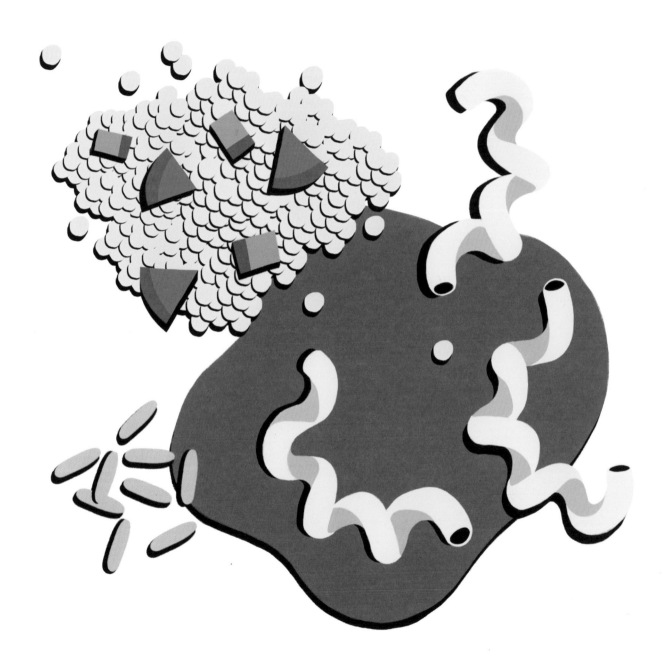

PASTA, RICE & COUSCOUS

PASTA, RICE & COUSCOUS

Pasta is a feeling as well as a fuel. Few plates are more eagerly awaited and satisfying than a bowl of hot pasta. You know how you are going to feel afterwards.

Pasta made from flour is a blend of protein and carbohydrate and, with the addition of a sauce containing protein such as a ragu, it will sustain you for a good few hours. Just remember, in Italy they serve small portions as it is eaten as a starter. Giancarlo and our son Giorgio were devastated when they were told they could no longer eat foods with gluten, but now we have found good brands of gluten-free dried pasta and we make our own fresh pasta (see page 147), so life has pretty much returned to normal.

Wheat was grown in Sicily before the Arab invasion. In fact, pasta was first introduced to Italy by the Arabs at the beginning of the 12th century, long before Marco Polo travelled to the East, which blows the myth that he brought the idea back to Venice. The term 'maccheroni' probably comes from the Sicilian word 'maccarruna', and it referred to short tubular pasta.

The first tomato sauce recipe dates from the late 18th century – a 1790 cookbook, *L'Apicio Moderno*. Before tomato sauce was added, pasta was eaten dry with the fingers. It was the liquid sauce that demanded the use of a fork.

Dried pasta and cooking instructions
Sicily exported huge amounts of dried pasta during the early Middle Ages. It is still mainly dried pasta that is eaten on the island rather than fresh. Dried pasta, these days, is extruded through metal dies, which means it is less absorbent than fresh pasta and is ideally suited to wetter sauces such as the Romanesco sauce on page 126 or the *Alla Norma* sauce on page 138.

To serve 4 as a main course or 6 as a starter use 320 g (11½ oz) pasta.

Cook the pasta in a large saucepan of salted boiling water according to the packet instructions until al dente. Always add the pasta to the sauce, which should be warmed through in a large frying pan. Toss to combine. The exception to this is when using an uncooked sauce such as pesto, which can be stirred through hot pasta in a bowl.

PESTO FROM TRAPANI

This makes a light, delicate sauce normally used for pasta but which is also good on fried fish or spread onto hot sourdough toast. This is the way our friend Marco Piraino prepares this traditional sauce. It is usually made without the aubergines (eggplants) but we loved the extra flavour and texture they offer. Use this sauce with fresh or dried pasta. In Sicily it is often served with the curly busiate pasta.

**Serves 6 as a main course or
8 as a starter**

---

850 g (1 lb 13 oz) fresh round tomatoes
100 g (3½ oz/⅔ cup) blanched almonds
seed oil for frying
1 aubergine (eggplant), cut into
   1 cm (½ in) cubes
1 garlic clove, peeled
salt and freshly ground black pepper
10 g (½ oz) Parmesan, finely grated
70 g (2¼ oz/scant 3 cups) basil leaves
150 ml (5 fl oz/⅔ cup) extra-virgin olive oil

Make a cross in the top of each tomatoe and then plunge them into a bowl of just-boiled water for a minute or two until the skins split. Remove from the hot water with a slotted spoon and plunge into a bowl of ice-cold water to cool for a few minutes. Meanwhile, blitz the almonds in a food processor to a gritty texture and heat enough seed oil to deep-fry the aubergine in a small saucepan. Fry the aubergine cubes until lightly browned and then remove from the oil with a slotted spoon. Set aside to drain on kitchen paper for a few minutes to cool.

Peel the skins from the tomatoes and discard the skins. Chop the flesh into small dice. Put the garlic, salt and pepper to taste, Parmesan, basil and olive oil together in a pestle and mortar. Grind until you have a rough paste, then add the almonds and tomatoes; give them a bash with the pestle then stir through. Add the aubergine last and stir to combine. Stir into hot cooked dried pasta, such as the busiate in the photo opposite (centre).

Above: Penne with
Sun-dried Tomato
& Chilli Relish.
Centre: Pesto from
Trapani. Below:
Pistachio Pesto.

PISTACHIO PESTO

We met a couple of passionate Sicilians selling jars of this in Ragusa Ibla. They told us you could fry some onion and bacon together and add the pistachio paste. You could also add it to a pan with sautéed prawns (shrimp), before adding pasta and little grated lemon zest. Or stir in a little cream to enrich it as a pasta sauce. I was sold and bought a jar. However, it is actually easy to make your own and you can alter the flavourings to suit. The best pistachios in Sicily come from the area of Bronte in the hills. I have found that the best flavour comes from the kind you shell at home, but I don't suggest you sit for hours slavishly picking them apart. However, a few of these, roughly chopped, on top of the pasta will enhance the taste and texture of the dish.

**Serves 4 (makes
approximately 225 g/8 oz)**

---

100 g (3½ oz/¾ cup) shelled unsalted
   pistachios
25 g (1 oz) parsley leaves and stalks
1 small garlic clove, peeled
salt and freshly ground black pepper
100 ml (3½ fl oz/scant ½ cup) extra-virgin
   olive oil
3 tablespoons lemon juice
25 g (1 oz) finely grated Parmesan

Put the pistachios into a food processor and grind to the texture of fine gravel. Add the remaining ingredients and whizz briefly again. Taste and adjust the seasoning. Use straight away, or store in the fridge covered with a thin layer of oil for up to a week. To use, stir into hot, just-cooked pasta (see photo on page 123).

ROMANESCO WITH PASTA

Broccolo here refers to those green pointed Romanesco cauliflowers that look like an incredible, miniature work of architecture. You can, however, make this sauce with white cauliflower – both types soften down to create a creamy pasta sauce (without any cream!). At Mandranova *agriturismo* near Agrigento, Silvia Di Vincenzo stirred the cauliflower into pasta shells. The shapes caught the soft florets with the *pinoli* (pine nuts) and tiny black currants. Local *pinoli* are long, fruity and oily, and have a distinct flavour a world apart from the tiny dry Chinese imported ones. Seek them out if you can.

This is supposed to be a sauce for pasta but for me it also makes the most delicious soupy stew to eat on a cold autumn day. To add a little crunch, you can top the dish with toasted breadcrumbs and a little grated hard cheese. Cooking the pasta in the *broccolo* water enhances the flavour, too.

Cut the Romanesco or cauliflower into florets and discard the leaves (you can use these too if you have lots of them). Plunge them into salted boiling water and cook until just tender when pierced with a fork. Get a large bowl of iced water ready. Remove the florets with a slotted spoon and drop them into the chilled water to cool and to keep their colour. Retain the cooking water.

Drain the Romanesco and use your hands to break the florets into smaller pieces. Heat the oil in a frying pan (skillet) and fry the onion and anchovies until just softened. Add the Romanesco, bay leaf, currants and pine nuts, then top up with the Romanesco cooking water to cover. Soften the saffron strands in a tablespoon of hot water and stir into the pan. Break up the Romanesco with a wooden spoon so that the sauce becomes dense and creamy. Taste and adjust the seasoning as necessary. Eat as it is or with cooked dried pasta, sprinkled with breadcrumbs or Parmesan, if you like.

Serves 4

---

500 g (1 lb 2 oz) Romanesco or white cauliflower
4 tablespoons extra-virgin olive oil
1 onion, finely chopped
3 anchovy fillets in oil, drained
1 bay leaf
1 tablespoon currants or small raisins
1 tablespoon pine nuts
pinch of saffron strands
salt and freshly ground black pepper
handful of dry breadcrumbs or finely grated Parmesan,
  to serve (optional)

QUICK BEEF RAGU

This meaty, as opposed to tomatoey, ragu makes the ideal filling for the *Arancine* on page 22 and is perfect with pasta too. Longer-cooking and fattier minced (ground) beef will give you a better, richer flavour, as the sauce concentrates, but when time is short this version is perfectly fine. *Estrattu* is a rich, concentrated tomato paste which is very important in Sicilian cooking. Many people still make their own in summer with the abundance of cheap, ripe tomatoes. You will see mounds of it for sale in the markets. Do bring some home and use it in place of tomato purée, but it is salty so be careful with additional seasoning.

Serves 8

---

4 tablespoons extra-virgin olive oil
1 carrot, finely chopped
1 celery stalk, finely chopped
1 onion, finely chopped
1 garlic clove, peeled and lightly crushed
500 g (1 lb 2 oz) lean minced (ground) beef
4 tablespoons tomato purée
   (tomato paste)
100 ml (3½ fl oz/scant ½ cup) full-bodied
   red wine such as Nero d'Avola
salt
small pinch of ground cloves

Heat the oil in a large saucepan and fry the carrot, celery, onion and garlic over a medium heat until softened, around 5 minutes. Add the minced beef and stir through for a couple of minutes, then add the tomato purée, red wine, two good pinches of salt and the ground cloves. Cook for around 10 minutes, stirring frequently with a wooden spoon to break up the meat. Taste and adjust the seasoning as necessary.

SLOW-COOKED PORK, BEEF & SAUSAGE RAGU

This is the opposite of the Quick Beef Ragu on page 131. Traditionally, ragu was made on a Sunday and normally it would be the mamma of the house who would get up early to get it started over a fire, so that it would be ready in time for a late lunch. Nowadays, with slow cookers and heavy, cast-iron casseroles like Le Creuset you can get it going, turn the oven on low and go out for the day. You will come back to a heavenly feast that is the wonderfully rich and sticky ragu ready to cling to pasta shapes or gnocchi.

We tested this recipe at our restaurant in Bray. A couple of the staff are Sicilian and they ate it for their dinner. They loved it and actually became quite emotional! I think we got pretty close to the original recipe. Don't worry if you don't have all the types of meat – it really should be made with what you have to hand, so use more beef or pork accordingly. Do try to find proper Italian sausages, though, as they are full of flavour from garlic, wine and sometimes fennel seeds and don't contain rusk. Serve this with dried or fresh long pasta.

Serves 8–10

425 g (15 oz) Italian sausages
325 g (11½ oz) pork spare ribs
425 g (15 oz) pork belly, cut into
    3 cm (1¼ in) cubes
425 g (15 oz) stewing beef, cut into
    8 cm (3¼ in) chunks
5 tablespoons extra-virgin olive oil
2 white or brown onions, finely chopped
3 garlic cloves, peeled and roughly
    chopped
2 bay leaves
1 sprig of rosemary
salt and freshly ground black pepper
300 ml (10 fl oz/1¼ cups) white or
    red wine
4 tablespoons tomato purée
    (tomato paste)
1.2 kg (2 lb 10 oz) tinned whole tomatoes,
    roughly chopped
1 litre (34 fl oz/4¼ cups) chicken, meat
    or vegetable stock, or hot water
6 potatoes (approximately 1 kg/2 lb 3 oz),
    peeled and cut in half
200 g (7 oz/1⅓ cups) peas, frozen or
    fresh (optional)

Brown the meat in batches in the oil in a large casserole dish over a medium heat, setting it aside in a large bowl when done. Add the onions to the pan in the remaining oil with the garlic, bay leaves, rosemary and seasoning and cook over a gentle heat to soften. It should take 7-10 minutes. Add the meat back into the pan with the wine and bring to the boil. Allow to reduce for few minutes. Add the tomato purée, tomatoes and stock and stir to combine.

Bring to the boil, then reduce the heat to a simmer and allow to cook slowly for 4–5 hours. The time will depend upon the cut of meat and the size. You need to cook it until the meat falls easily from the bones. Add the potatoes after around 4 hours and continue to cook until they are cooked through. Add the peas, if using, towards the end of the cooking time. Cook for 15 minutes if using frozen peas and 30 minutes if using fresh ones. Taste and adjust the seasoning as necessary.

Eat the stew as it is or ladle off most of the sauce and serve it with pasta, followed by the meat and potatoes as a main course served with the Purple Sprouting Broccoli from page 104.

SAUSAGE & WILD FENNEL RAGU

Wild fennel grows everywhere but most of us ignore it. It sprouts up merrily in early spring in the UK; it is bright green and feathery, then becomes darker over the months and finally blossoms into yellow flowers that yield the seeds in autumn. Do seek it out; you can usually find it in hedgerows. Fresh ricotta is often stirred into hot pasta in Sicily; sometimes it can be dry, in which case stir through a little cream at the same time.

Serves 4 as a main course or 6 as a starter

4 tablespoons extra-virgin olive oil
½ large leek (about 150 g/5 oz), trimmed and finely chopped
500 g (1 lb 2 oz) Italian rusk-free sausages
5 tablespoons red wine
small handful (25 g/1 oz) of wild fennel, finely chopped, or 1 teaspoon fennel seeds
salt and freshly ground black pepper
100 g (3½ oz/generous ⅓ cup) ricotta
75 ml (2½ fl oz/⅓ cup) double (heavy) cream (optional)
25 g (1 oz) finely grated Parmesan (optional)

Heat the oil in a large frying pan and fry the leek for around 5 minutes. Meanwhile, squeeze the sausage meat from the skins and crumble it into the pan with the leek. Fry over a medium to low heat until the meat is browned. Add the red wine and let it evaporate for around 5 minutes, then stir in the wild fennel (keep a little for garnish) and some pepper. Let the ragu cook slowly over a low heat for around 30 minutes. Taste and add a little salt if necessary (Italian sausages tend to be quite salty so go easy). Just before serving, stir in the ricotta and cream, if using, then add just-cooked pasta to the pan. Stir through and serve garnished with the reserved fennel and, if liked, some Parmesan on top.

FISH SAUCE

Use a mixture of fish, as each one will impart its own flavour. In Palermo there was a fishmonger who had a large marble slab covered in tiny or broken fish, the kind of scraps that would be perfect for this dish. By 10.30 a.m. the slab was cleared and the Sicilians were on their way home with bags of cheap fish for a tasty ragu. Since we don't have a fishmonger near our home, I put a few shell-on prawns (shrimp) into the sauce to give it a stronger flavour. This sauce is best with dried pasta such as spaghetti.

**Serves 4 as a main course
or 6 as a starter**

---

4 tablespoons extra-virgin olive oil,
  plus extra to drizzle
1 shallot, finely chopped
1 carrot, finely chopped
1 celery stalk from the heart with
  some leaves, finely chopped
1 garlic clove, peeled and finely chopped
1 bay leaf
a few parsley stalks, finely chopped
5 large raw prawns (shrimp), shells and
  heads on if possible
200 g (7 oz/1 cup) tinned whole tomatoes,
  chopped
pinch of chilli flakes
300 ml (10 fl oz/1¼ cups) fish, shellfish
  or vegetable stock, or water
500 g (1 lb 2 oz) mixed flavourful white fish
  such as sea bass, sea bream, sole
salt and freshly ground black pepper
320 g (11 oz/3 cups) pasta of your choice,
  to serve
small handful of parsley, finely chopped,

Heat the oil in a large saucepan and fry the shallot, carrot, celery and garlic with the bay leaf and parsley stalks over a low heat for 5 minutes. Peel the prawns and discard the shells. Remove the heads and set aside. Add the tomatoes, chilli and prawn heads, if using, followed by the stock, to the pan and bring to the boil. Let it cook slowly for 10 minutes. Use tongs to fish out the prawn heads and squeeze the juices out into the pan. Discard the heads. Add the fish and the prawns to the pan and cook slowly for 15 minutes. Taste and adjust the seasoning as necessary.

Toss freshly cooked and drained pasta with the sauce in a large frying pan and add a drizzle of olive oil and a little parsley. Serve straight away.

PASTA WITH AUBERGINE & TOMATOES

This glorious pasta dish was made to honour Vincenzo Bellini, the composer of the opera *Norma*, who was born in Catania in 1801. It ticks all the boxes for an outstanding dish in Sicilian cuisine; short, bouncy pasta is tossed with crispy-edged aubergine (eggplant), sweet tomato sauce, basil and salty ricotta cheese. I have used coarsely grated feta as I can't find *ricotta salata* in my local shops, but do seek it out online or in Italian delis. It has a crumbly texture and a tangy flavour. This is the way chef Roberto Toro cooked his *Pasta alla Norma* at the stunning Belmond Grand Hotel Timeo in Taormina.

> **Serves 4 as a main course
> or 6 as a starter**

1 small shallot, peeled but left whole
2 fat garlic cloves, peeled and crushed
1 sprig of basil, plus a small handful of basil leaves
    to garnish
3 tablespoons extra-virgin olive oil
1 × 400 g (14 oz) tin cherry tomatoes or 400 g (14 oz)
    fresh, blanched and peeled tomatoes
salt and freshly ground black pepper
1 teaspoon caster (superfine) sugar, optional
seed oil for deep-frying
1 large aubergine (eggplant), topped and tailed and cut
    into 2 cm (¾ in) cubes
320 g (11 oz/3 cups) pasta such as penne or spaghetti

To serve
100g (3 ½ oz/⅔ cup) feta cheese, coarsely grated
few extra basil leaves
extra-virgin olive oil
freshly ground black pepper

Put the shallot, garlic cloves, basil sprig and olive oil together in a pan and heat gently for a couple of minutes until you can smell the flavourings. Add the tomatoes to the pan and continue to cook gently for around 20 minutes. Season to taste with salt and pepper and a little sugar if the tomatoes are too acidic.

Meanwhile, heat the seed oil to around 175°C (350°F) and fry the aubergine cubes until golden. This will only take a few minutes. Scoop out the aubergines with a slotted spoon and drain on kitchen paper.

Put the pasta on to cook in a large pan of boiling well-salted water. Cook until tender according to the manufacturer's suggestions. Remove the onion and garlic from the oil and discard. Add the aubergines to the sauce and stir through gently.

Add the cooked, drained pasta and stir or toss again to combine. Serve in warm bowls with the feta, a few extra basil leaves, a swirl of olive oil and a twist of black pepper.

Roasted aubergines:
If you prefer not to deep-fry the aubergines, preheat the oven to 200°C (400°F/Gas 6). Toss the aubergines in a large bowl with 3 tablespoons of the olive oil and seasoning. Pour onto a tray lined with baking parchment and spread out well so they aren't piled up or they will steam. Put into the oven to roast for around 30 minutes or until they appear lightly crisp and golden brown. Add to the tomato sauce as before.

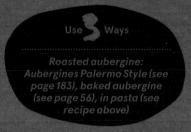

Use Ways

*Roasted aubergine:
Aubergines Palermo Style (see page 183), baked aubergine (see page 56), in pasta (see recipe above)*

SARDINE & WILD FENNEL SAUCE

Pasta *con le sarde* is almost a national dish in Sicily and is found in various forms all over the island. It is indeed a recipe that serves up a rich, splendid plate of history, showing Arab and Italian traditions together. The typical pasta to eat with it is busiate, twirls of pasta made from semolina flour (see page 122) but spaghetti is a good substitute. This recipe is from passionate foodie Caterina, owner of Il Palladio hotel and restaurant in Giardini Naxos. She uses abundant handfuls of wild fennel and local sardines. In the UK, wild fennel grows both in gardens and in the countryside, so do seek it out. If you can't find it, use fresh dill instead. If you can get hold of the long, Italian pine nuts, they add flavour as well as crunch to the pasta. They are expensive but if you are travelling in Sicily they are widely available at the markets.

**Serves 4 as a main course
or 6 as a starter**

---

1 white onion, finely chopped
1 garlic clove, peeled and roughly
  chopped
a little fresh red chilli or a pinch of dried
  chilli flakes, to taste
6 tablespoons extra-virgin olive oil
large handful of wild fennel
5 anchovies in oil, drained
1 heaped tablespoon pine nuts
2 tablespoons soft, sweet raisins
  or currants
handful of cherry tomatoes, roughly
  chopped
salt and freshly ground black pepper
10 fresh sardines, filleted
good pinch of saffron strands
320 g (11 oz) spaghetti
handful of toasted flaked almonds,
  roughly crushed

Fry the onion, garlic and chilli together in the oil until soft. Boil the wild fennel whole for 5 minutes and save the water to cook your pasta later. Squeeze the fennel to get rid of the excess water and chop finely. Melt the anchovies in the oil with the onion and add the pine nuts, raisins, fennel and tomatoes. Season to taste.

Add the sardines and the saffron mixed with 2 tablespoons of hot water, cover and leave to cook for 5 minutes or until the fish is cooked through. Break the fish up a little and taste the sauce. Season as necessary. Boil the reserved fennel water in a large pan and add the spaghetti. Cook until tender according to the manufacturer's suggestions and drain. Add just-cooked pasta to the sauce and toss to combine. Serve in warm bowls topped with the almonds.

SPAGHETTI WITH ANCHOVIES, CAPERS & CHERRY TOMATOES

This quick-to-cook pasta dish appears in various guises all over the island. It is made from ingredients that you normally have to hand and never fails to please. This recipe is from Stefano Gegnacorsi, the hard-working general manager of the Belmond Grand Hotel Timeo in Taormina. He told us that after a busy day at the hotel this is what he goes home to cook. Try to find small capers sold in salt and give them a good rinse – the best ones come from the sunny island of Pantelleria.

**Serves 4 as a main course
or 6 as a starter**

1 onion, finely chopped
25 g (1 oz) anchovy fillets, fresh or tinned
   in oil, drained
2 tablespoons extra-virgin olive oil
400 g (14 oz) cherry tomatoes,
   cut into quarters
handful of olives, pitted
3 tablespoons small capers in salt,
   well rinsed
salt and freshly ground black pepper
320 g (11½ oz) durum wheat spaghetti
a little strong extra-virgin olive oil,
   to serve
3 tablespoons finely chopped parsley,
   to garnish
a handful of olives, pitted

Prepare the sauce by sautéing the onion with the anchovies in a little of their oil and the olive oil over a low heat for up to 10 minutes or until softened, but make sure they don't take on any colour. Add the cherry tomatoes, olives and capers to the pan and season to taste. You may not need any salt as the anchovies are already salty.

Put the pasta on to cook in a large saucepan of boiling salted water. Cook until tender, according to the packet instructions.

Add the just-cooked and drained pasta to the sauce and toss, allowing a little of the pasta water to fall into the pan – this will help to dilute and emulsify the sauce. Finish with a swirl of your best peppery extra-virgin olive oil, a scattering of parsley and the olives. Serve in warm bowls.

Use 3 Ways

risotto, soup,
*timballo (see
page 158)*

CHERRY TOMATO SAUCE

I learnt to make this sauce from our Sicilian head chef Gregorio Piazza. He showed me how he leaves the stalks on the tomatoes during cooking as they add a wonderful grassy flavour to the sauce.

Buy tomatoes when they are really ripe, dark red and soft. In Sicily, tomatoes are available all year round but they are much better in the sunnier months. Taste them to make sure you are happy with the sweetness. *Datterini* are tiny plum tomatoes that are perfect for this. However, if you find your tomato sauce is not sweet enough add a little sugar to taste. This recipe can also be made with tinned cherry or San Marzano plum tomatoes, which contain little water.

This sauce has infinite uses and is used in several recipes in this book, from the risotto on page 154, to the *timballo* on page 158 and more, and can be used in place of the *sfincione* sauce on page 33.

Makes approximately 1 kg (2 lb 3 oz)

---

1 carrot, roughly chopped
1 celery stalk, roughly chopped
1 white onion, roughly chopped
5 tablespoons extra-virgin olive oil
1 kg (2 lb 3 oz) cherry tomatoes on the vine
   or 1.2 kg (2 lb 10 oz) tinned cherry or
   whole plum tomatoes
1 sprig of basil
1 teaspoon salt
freshly ground black pepper, to taste
1–2 teaspoons sugar (optional)

Fry the carrot, celery and onion in the olive oil in a large saucepan over a medium heat for around 10 minutes or until soft. Add the tomatoes with a few of their stalks (if using fresh) to the pan with the basil and seasoning and cook over a medium heat with a lid on. Stir frequently, bashing the tomatoes with a potato masher to break them up. Bring to the boil, then remove the lid and reduce the heat to a low simmer and cook for around 30–40 minutes. Check the seasoning and adjust as necessary, adding a teaspoon of sugar if the tomatoes still taste acidic. Use the sauce as it is or remove the basil and stalks and use a stick blender to blend the sauce to a smooth, velvety consistency.

FRESH PASTA

The general universal pasta recipe is: 1 egg to 100 g (3½ oz/scant 1 cup) '00' flour. In Sicily and the south of Italy the flour used is finely ground *semola*, semolina flour. This is a type of flour which, unlike pure white flour, also contains a little of the bran from around the outside of the wheat kernel, giving it a slightly creamy pale yellow colour. Ideally, the pasta is rolled on a wooden surface, as the tiny particles of wood that project from the surface add texture, helping the pasta to absorb the sauce that will eventually coat it. Many Italians use a tablecloth for the same purpose. To save time, the pasta dough can be made in a food processor, which is particularly useful when making coloured pasta as the blades distribute the colour evenly and quickly.

Makes enough pasta for 4 as a main course or 6 as a starter

---

200 g (7 oz/1⅔ cups) '00' or very fine
 semolina flour, plus a little extra
 if necessary
2 eggs (preferably corn-fed for colour)

Pour the flour into a bowl and make a well in the centre. Crack the eggs into the well. Using a table knife, gradually mix the flour into the eggs. Keep mixing the eggs and flour together until they form a thick paste.

Use the fingertips of one hand to incorporate the rest of the flour and form a ball of dough. Discard the dry little crumbs. The dough should form a soft but firm, flexible ball. If it is still sticking to the palm of your hand, add a little more flour – but be careful to stop adding flour as soon as it stops sticking. If it's really dry and has many cracks, add a drop or two of water – do this in a bowl or the food processor.

Knead the pasta for 5–10 minutes, or until it springs back to the touch, the colour is uniform and, when cut open, the ball of dough is full of small air bubbles; this means you have kneaded it for long enough. Leave the pasta to 'rest' for at least 20 minutes or up to 1 day, lightly dusted with flour and wrap it in cling film (plastic wrap) to prevent it from drying out while it rests.

LONG PASTA

Follow the recipe for Fresh Pasta on page 145. After the resting time the pasta can be rolled out with a rolling pin or a pasta machine. To make any of the long pasta such as tagliatelle or pappardelle by hand, roll the pasta out using a heavy wooden rolling pin. Lightly dust the surface of the table, the pasta and the rolling pin with flour to prevent it sticking.

When it is very thin (about 1 mm thick) and you can see your fingers through it, it is ready. Dust the work surface and the pasta with plenty of flour again to prevent it sticking to itself. Gently fold over one short edge, making a flap of about 3 cm (1¼ in). Now do the same with the other short edge. Fold the edges over again and again, sprinkling flour over the surface to stop the dough sticking to itself. Stop when the folded edges meet in the middle. Cut across the folds into the desired thicknesses to make the *pasta lunga*, the thinnest being tagliolini and the fattest pappardelle. Slide a long knife underneath the centre, matching the blunt edge of the knife to where the two folded edges come together. Hold and twist the knife in the air and the pasta ribbons will fall down in cut lengths either side.

When cut, pull out into individual strands and toss with coarse semolina or a little more flour. Don't pile the pasta high but leave it in a single layer or the weight will cause it to stick together. Cook within the hour. The cooking time should be 2–3 minutes, or until al dente, in a pan of boiling salted water.

GLUTEN-FREE FRESH PASTA

Finally, after being diagnosed with gluten intolerance, Giancarlo and Giorgio can enjoy their favourite bowl of fresh pasta once more. We started working with different flours and xantham gum to achieve a pasta that tasted good and didn't fall apart in the water. It also has a bite to it like pasta made with conventional '00' flour. We don't add salt to our dough as we cook the pasta in well-salted water.

Makes enough pasta for 4 as a main course or 6 as a starter

---

3 eggs
50 g (2 oz/generous ¼ cup) white or brown rice flour
50 g (2 oz/generous ⅓ cup) buckwheat flour
175 g (6 oz/scant 1½ cups) tapioca flour (tapioca starch)
1 teaspoon xantham gum
1 tablespoon extra-virgin olive oil

Crack the eggs into a measuring jug and beat with a fork. They should measure around 180 ml (6¼ fl oz) – if not, add a couple of tablespoons of water to the jug. Put the eggs with all the other ingredients into a food processor and blend until a ball of dough forms. If it is very dry and doesn't form a ball, add another tablespoon of water. You are aiming for a firm but pliable dough. Knead the dough for a few minutes to ensure it is well blended. Wrap in cling film (plastic wrap) and rest for 30 minutes at room temperature, or if you prefer to keep it longer it can be left up to a day in the fridge.

If you don't have a food processor, tip the dry ingredients into a bowl and stir to combine. Make a well in the centre of the ingredients and crack the eggs into it with the oil and 2 tablespoons of water. Use a table knife to break up the eggs and combine the dry ingredients little by little. Eventually your knife will become ineffective, so use your hands to bring the dough together into a ball. If it is very dry and hard add a tablespoon more water. Knead and rest the dough as above.

After the dough has rested use as fresh pasta, rolling the dough by hand or through a machine, remembering to use gluten-free flour for dusting.

SUNSET AGNOLOTTI STUFFED WITH SEA BASS

In summer, at our friend Mimmo's wonderful restaurant Osteria Bacchus in Sant'Ambrogio, guests can sit opposite the restaurant on a terrace overlooking the bay of Cefalù. They can enjoy this vibrant pasta dish for dinner, with its vivid colours reflecting those of the sunset.

**Serves 4 as a main course
or 6 as a starter
(makes 35–40 shapes)**

For the pasta
200 g (7 oz/1⅔ cups) '00' or very fine
   semolina flour, plus a little extra
   if necessary
2 eggs (preferably corn-fed for colour),
   plus beaten egg to seal the agnolotti
2 tablespoons tomato purée
   (tomato paste)
pinch of saffron powder, mixed with
   1 teaspoon hot water

For the stuffing
1 onion, finely chopped
1 large garlic clove, peeled and
   finely chopped
2 tablespoons extra-virgin olive oil
2 teaspoons pink peppercorns
3 sea bass or sea bream fillets, or any
   other flavourful white fish
   (approximately 450 g/1 lb)
2 tablespoons lemon juice
finely grated zest of 1 small lemon
salt, to taste

For the sauce
100 g (3½ oz/scant ½ cup) salted butter
small handful of sage leaves
few slices red chilli, according to taste
3 garlic cloves, skins left on and lightly
   crushed
salt and freshly ground black pepper
4 tablespoons Fish Broth (see page 163)
   or cooking water

Divide the flour between two bowls and crack an egg into each one. Add the tomato purée to one bowl and the saffron water to the other. Follow the instructions for making fresh pasta on page 145, adding a little more flour as necessary to make two firm balls of dough. Now take half of each ball of coloured pasta and use your hands or a food processor to blend the two halves together. You will now have three balls of pasta – an orange one, a yellow one and a yellowy-orange one. Cover all three with cling film (plastic wrap) and rest for 20 minutes at room temperature.

Meanwhile, make the stuffing. Gently fry the onion and garlic in the olive oil until soft. Add the pink peppercorns, lightly crushing them with your fingers as you drop them in. Add the fish to the pan skin-side up to begin with. Cook for 5 minutes, then turn skin-side down and cook for a couple more minutes until tender. Add the lemon juice, zest and salt. Transfer to a large plate. Peel the skin from the fish and discard. Use a fork to mash the flesh to a rough paste. Leave to cool.

Line up the three balls of pasta in a row and roll them out with a large rolling pin at the same time, dusting them lightly with flour every now and again. Gradually, the three colours will blend together into soft stripes. This can also be done in a pasta machine: divide each ball of pasta into three, then roll each piece into small, walnut-sized balls. You will end up with nine balls. Take three different-coloured balls at a time and roll them together. Feed this into your pasta machine and blended lengths of coloured dough will appear.

Roll the pasta very thin (around 1 mm thick) and, using a pastry cutter or a large wine glass, cut the pasta into circles around 9 cm (3½ in) across. Put a heaped teaspoon of filling onto the pasta circles and brush a little of the beaten egg around the edge of one half. Fold the circles around the filling and press the edges together to form a half-moon shape. Expel the air from inside as you do this.

Cook the agnolotti in boiling salted water for 4–6 minutes, until al dente. Meanwhile, make the sauce by melting the butter in a large frying pan. Add the sage, chilli and garlic and season. When the agnolotti are done, drain and add to the sauce in the pan with the broth or cooking water. Shake the pan to combine the water and butter. Serve immediately in warmed bowls or plates.

RAVIOLI STUFFED WITH RICOTTA & LEMON

We watched the experienced hands of Valentina (opposite) – the pasta maker at Taverna Nicastro in Modica – work her magic on a huge sheet of bright yellow pasta. Between the rhythmic movements of flouring, rolling, filling, folding and cutting, she produced puffy parcels of lemon-scented ricotta wrapped in pasta. It was a joy to watch the timing and carefully choreographed kitchen performance of the cooks. In many restaurants this lemony pasta is served with a pork ragu, which is actually just the sauce from the traditional slow-cooked ragu like the one on page 133. It is also good with the Cherry Tomato Sauce on page 144, or simply tossed in butter and sage like the Sunset Agnolotti on page 149.

**Serves 4 as a main course or
6 as a starter (makes 25–30 ravioli)**

1 quantity of Fresh Pasta (see page 145)
coarse semolina or '00' flour,
    for dusting
1 quantity of Cherry Tomato Sauce
    (see page 144) or the sauce from the
    Slow-Cooked Ragu (see page 133)
a little of your best extra-virgin olive oil,
    to serve

For the filling
250 g (9 oz/1 cup) ricotta
finely grated zest of ½–1 lemon,
    plus extra to serve
salt and freshly ground black pepper
½ teaspoon freshly grated nutmeg

Start by making the filling. Drain the ricotta then combine all the ingredients together in a bowl. Go easy on the lemon zest as it can be quite overpowering, but season to suit your taste. This is very important as you want the flavour to shine through the pasta and sauce.

Bring a large pan of salted water two-thirds full to the boil.

To make the ravioli, roll out half the fresh pasta, keeping the other half wrapped in cling film (plastic wrap). Dust the work surface with flour, but don't dust the top side of the pasta or it will be hard to seal. Roll out the pasta using a rolling pin or a pasta machine until you can see your hand through it. Set the machine on the second to last setting – the very last setting makes the thinnest pasta but this is often too fragile for ravioli.

Now dot a heaped teaspoon of the filling at even intervals (two fingers-width apart is ideal) on to a sheet of pasta and place another sheet of the same length over the top. Press down around the filling to expel the air and seal the pasta sheets together. Using a pasta wheel or a sharp knife, cut the ravioli into even 5 cm (2 in) squares. Set the shapes aside on a surface dusted with flour or semolina (semolina is good as it doesn't stick to the pasta).

Cook the ravioli in the boiling water for 4–6 minutes, until al dente – test by trying the edge of one. Warm your chosen sauce in a large frying pan and toss the just-cooked ravioli into it, allowing a little pasta water to fall into the sauce as they are added. Shake the pan to amalgamate the water and sauce. Serve immediately in warmed bowls or plates with a little lemon zest grated over the top and a swirl of your best olive oil.

RICE

There is an ancient history to rice production in Sicily. It was probably introduced there before the rest of Italy by the Arabs through the thriving trading port of Alexandria, where one of the entrances was named 'Pepper Gate' in recognition of the important trade in spices. Rice was written about in Roman times, but was used for medicinal purposes only. During my research our teacher friend Giuseppe Mazzarella sent me a very old Sicilian recipe called *risu ca minnulata*: the rice is cooked in almond milk with a little salt until tender and served with a sprinkling of ground almonds on top. It has a delicate but moreish flavour and was traditionally given to people when they were unwell. It is lovely and I think even better finished off with a swirl of honey.

The 9th century Arab scholar al-Asma'i said, 'White rice with melted butter and white sugar is not of this world' – meaning that it surely came from paradise. Rice was originally a rare and exotic foodstuff, but gradually it became accessible to everyone.

CHERRY TOMATO RISOTTO

This bright orange risotto packs a flavour punch thanks to Sicily's famous cherry tomatoes.
I recommend making this when you see Italian cherry tomatoes, known as *datterini*, in the shops.
The risotto is pretty to look at and should be served in small amounts as it is filling. This is a recipe from
Monaci delle Terre Nere, a beautiful hotel on the slopes of Mount Etna.

When you are making risotto, it helps to have everything you need within reach, so that you don't
have to leave it unattended while you find the cheese from the back of the fridge or discover you
have run out of wine. Have your heated stock ready in a pot by your risotto pan with a ladle to hand.

Serves 4

---

2 tablespoons extra-virgin olive oil,
    plus extra to serve
50 g (2 oz/½ stick) butter
1 white onion, finely chopped
1 celery stalk, finely chopped
fine salt and freshly ground black pepper
300 g (10½ oz/1⅓ cups) carnaroli
    or other risotto rice
100 ml (3½ fl oz/scant ½ cup) white wine
700–750 ml (24–25 fl oz/3 cups)
    hot chicken, ham or vegetable stock,
    or hot water
500 g (1 lb 2 oz) Cherry Tomato Sauce
    (see page 144)
50 g (2 oz) Parmesan, finely grated
125 g (4 oz) ball of buffalo mozzarella,
    drained and roughly torn
a few small basil leaves, to garnish

Heat the oil and half the butter in a large saucepan – the oil
helps to stop the butter burning. When the butter has melted,
soften the onion and celery with some salt and pepper over
a low heat for around 10 minutes.

Add the rice to the pan and allow it to toast for 3–5 minutes,
stirring constantly, until all the grains are covered in the butter
and oil. Pour in the wine and allow to evaporate for 2–3 minutes.

Ladle in around 500 ml (17 fl oz/2¼ cups) of the stock and
the tomato sauce and mix quickly into the rice. Stir frequently,
keeping the heat medium-low. When the risotto thickens to the
point where you can see the bottom of the pan when you draw
the spoon across it, add another ladleful of stock.

After about 20 minutes taste the risotto to see whether it
is done. The rice grains should be clear on the outside but still
have a little white centre; they should feel soft on the outside
with a hint of firmness in the centre. Adjust the seasoning to
taste. Remove the pan from the heat. It is better to leave it
slightly soupy as the liquid will continue to be absorbed over
the following few minutes.

Beat in the remaining butter and the Parmesan – this will
make your risotto creamy. Cover the pan and allow the risotto
to rest for 3–5 minutes. Serve in warmed shallow bowls with
a swirl of good olive oil, the mozzarella, a twist of black pepper
and a few small basil leaves.

ORANGE & BASIL RISOTTO

This sublime risotto takes inspiration from the fabulous sweet oranges and intensely flavoured herbs that grow in Etna's fertile soil and under the Sicilian sun. Do serve swirled with your best extra-virgin olive oil and garnished with the basil – the marriage of flavours is a joy.

Serves 4

---

50 g (2 oz/½ stick) salted butter
2 tablespoons extra-virgin olive oil,
   plus extra to serve
1 shallot, finely chopped
300 g (10½ oz/1⅓ cups) Arborio
   or carnaroli rice
100 ml (3½ fl oz/scant ½ cup) white wine
juice and finely grated zest of
   1 large orange
1–1.2 litres (34–41 fl oz/4¼–5 cups)
   hot chicken or vegetable stock
50 g (2 oz) Parmesan, finely grated
salt, to taste
small handful of basil leaves, roughly torn,
   to garnish

Follow the instructions for the Cherry Tomato Risotto (see page 154), substituting the tomato sauce with the zest and juice of the orange and adding the extra stock. Serve in warm bowls, drizzled with a good olive oil and garnished with a few torn or small basil leaves.

RICE TIMBALE

Salvatore, our guide around Palermo, likened Sicilian culture to lasagne, with each layer a different layer of history. You can take a bite from the lasagne but you cannot separate the layers; you bite into them all together. It is the same with the Sicilian dish of *timballo*, named after the timbale, the mould it is cooked in.

Rice timbale is an elaborate layered dish from eastern Sicily, which is said to derive from Catania during the time of the Arab occupation. There are probably hundreds of variations of timbale; some are made with penne and I have seen ones made with spaghetti. In fact, it is a good way to use up leftover risotto or pasta. And do try layers of roasted aubergine (eggplant), flavouring the rice with saffron or adding cooked mushrooms, for a few ideas. I spent a day working with our chef Gregorio Piazza from Augusta, near Catania, and we invented our own version, taking into account our children's preferences and what we thought people would realistically make at home. It is gluten-free and can be adapted to a filling of your choice. Gregorio said proudly that it looks British but it tastes Sicilian! Our children love it and it is not complicated to make. You can leave it in an ovenproof dish or go for the 'wow' factor and cook the timbale in a cake tin, which can be removed after cooking.

Serves 8–10

---

5 tablespoons extra-virgin olive oil
50 g (2 oz/½ stick) salted butter
1 shallot or white onion, finely chopped
500 g (1 lb 2 oz/2¼ cups) Arborio rice
200 ml (7 fl oz/scant 1 cup) white wine
550 g (1 lb 3 oz) Cherry Tomato Sauce
  (see page 144)
800–900 ml (28–31 fl oz/3⅓–4 cups)
  hot chicken or vegetable stock,
  or hot water
100 g (3½ oz) grana padano, finely grated
salt and freshly ground black pepper
4 × 125 g (4 oz) balls of mozzarella
400 g (14 oz/2 cups) squeezed out
  spinach (from approximately 1 kg/
  2 lb 3 oz fresh leaves or 500 g/1 lb 2 oz
  frozen spinach)
1 garlic clove, peeled and lightly crushed
handful of basil leaves

Preheat the oven to 180°C (350°F/Gas 4). Heat 3 tablespoons of the oil and the butter in a frying pan and fry the shallot until soft, then add the rice. Toast the rice for around 3 minutes – it will start to crackle – then add the wine. Allow the wine to evaporate and reduce for another 3 minutes, then add the tomato sauce and 600 ml (20 fl oz/2½ cups) of the stock. Stir through frequently, keeping the heat to medium, and add a little more stock as necessary until you have a firm, thick risotto, which should take around 20 minutes. Add 80 g (3 oz) of the Grana Padano and stir through. Season to taste and remove from the heat.

Cut the mozzarella into 1 cm (½ in) slices and put into a colander to drain. Sauté the spinach in the remaining oil flavoured with the garlic and seasoned with salt and pepper to taste. Set aside.

Spread half of the tomatoey rice in the bottom of a 30 x 21 cm (12 x 8¼ in) ovenproof dish at least 5 cm (2 in) deep. Then add the spinach, followed by a layer of mozzarella and half of the Grana Padano. Follow this with the basil leaves, the remaining rice and top with the rest of the grana padano. Bake in the oven for 20 minutes. Serve straight away, while the cheese is still bubbling on top.

Variation: This timbale recipe also makes a beautiful layered savoury cake when cooked in a cake tin. To do this, generously grease a loose-bottomed 24 cm (9½ in) cake tin with butter. Follow the method above and after removing from the oven allow the timbale to sit for 10 minutes before removing from the tin.

COUSCOUS

Couscous, or *cuscus*, is Arab-Sicilian cuisine and is found mainly on the western, the Arab, side of the island. There is a whole festival dedicated to it in San Vito Lo Capo at the end of summer, when chefs come from around the world to be judged on their vats of fluffy couscous and richly scented broths. Sicilian couscous is usually made with fish and contains bay leaves, whereas the typically North African couscous is made with lamb and spices, but these days there are many crossovers.

Couscous is made from the action of stirring and rolling semolina flour and water together with your hands in large dish called a *mafaradda*. I remember making it with an experienced friend of ours, Nonna Giovanna, who cooked her couscous in a *couscoussière*, an old yellow earthenware pot with small holes in the bottom and the lid, which sits over a pan of boiling broth. The lid was sealed up with a length of dough to prevent the steam from escaping, forcing it through the couscous instead.

The tiny pasta grains are steamed for around 45 minutes. The broth can be made from fish or lamb and is filtered and used to pour over the couscous at the table. Normally the fish for the broth isn't eaten, but the filtered broth can be used to cook filleted fish just before serving, which are then wonderfully tasty and can be spooned on top of the couscous. Since making couscous from scratch takes dedication, our recipes use precooked couscous instead, which simply needs to be revived in hot stock for 5 minutes.

You can make twice the quantity of stock you need and freeze the rest for next time. This makes it quite quick to throw together and is good for entertaining. Nowadays you can buy maize couscous or use quinoa instead, which is good for a gluten-free diet.

FISH & SHELLFISH CousCous

In Italy, they often use small or damaged fish, or the bones of particular kinds like scorpion fish, John Dory or gurnards, as these all have a good strong flavour to impart to a stock. These types of fish aren't always easy to find, so I add the heads and shells of prawns (shrimp) instead. You can use a bought fish stock for this which is a lot easier but doesn't have the flavour of a homemade one. If you do buy one, bump up the flavour by adding the cinnamon, chilli, wine and tomato purée from the recipe below.

Serves 6–8

For the fish broth
2 tablespoons extra-virgin olive oil
1 onion, finely chopped
1 celery stalk, finely chopped
1 carrot, finely chopped
1 kg (2 lb 3 oz) mixed fish heads and bones
    and prawn (shrimp) heads and shells
3 garlic cloves, peeled and lightly crushed
1 bay leaf
1 small cinnamon stick
½–1 red chilli, finely sliced
4 tablespoons white wine
3 tablespoons tomato purée
    (tomato paste)
2 litres (68 fl oz/8½ cups) tepid water

For the couscous
1 small garlic clove, peeled and
    finely grated
5 tablespoons extra-virgin olive oil
25 g (1 oz/¼ cup) toasted chopped
    or flaked almonds
finely grated zest of ½ orange
finely grated zest of ½ lemon
pinch of ground cinnamon
1 teaspoon ground cumin
300 g (10½ oz/1⅔ cups) wheat
    or maize couscous
large handful of parsley, chopped
large handful of mint leaves, chopped

Fish for the filtered broth
1.5 kg (3 lb 5 oz) cleaned and scaled
    mixed fish such as sea bream, sea bass,
    king prawns (jumbo shrimp)
1–2 teaspoons salt

First make the fish broth. Heat the oil in a large saucepan and fry the onion, celery and carrot for 10 minutes or until softened. Add the fish heads and bones, prawn heads and shells, garlic, bay leaf, cinnamon and chilli according to taste and stir through. Add the wine and allow to reduce for a few minutes then stir in the tomato purée and water and cook for around 30 minutes.

Meanwhile, put the ingredients for the couscous, apart from the herbs, into a heatproof bowl and stir together.

Cut the fish into 5–8 cm (2–3¼ in) pieces.

Strain the broth through a fine sieve and pour into a saucepan. Season to taste with the salt and a little more chilli, if you like. Prepare the couscous by pouring over the hot broth following the amounts given for hot water on the packet. You should still have some broth leftover. Stir into the couscous and allow it to sit for 5 minutes, then fluff it up with a fork and add the fresh herbs.

Meanwhile, cook the fish pieces with the king prawns in the remaining hot broth until cooked through – this will take only 7–10 minutes, depending on the size of your fish and prawns. Serve the couscous on a warm serving platter accompanied by the fish broth and fish in a bowl with a ladle for guests to help themselves.

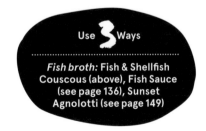

Use **3** Ways

Fish broth: Fish & Shellfish Couscous (above), Fish Sauce (see page 136), Sunset Agnolotti (see page 149)

QUINOA & LAMB COUSCOUS STYLE

It is good to use inexpensive cuts of lamb or mutton for this recipe. They impart a delicious flavour and stand up to the long cooking time. This is more of an Arab-style dish as it uses lamb and spices. We used quinoa as it is gluten-free but do use wheat or maize couscous instead, if you prefer. The first stage of this recipe essentially cooks the lamb and potatoes but also provides a stock. The couscous (or in our case quinoa) is then cooked in some of the stock and the lamb and potatoes are served in the rest of it.

Serves 6–8

2 tablespoons extra-virgin olive oil
500 g (1 lb 2 oz) lamb breast, neck or ribs, cut into 6 pieces
1 celery stalk, roughly chopped
2 carrots, peeled and left whole
1 onion, cut into quarters
1 garlic clove, peeled
1 sprig of rosemary
small handful of parsley
1 teaspoon fennel seeds
1 teaspoon coriander seeds
1 apple, cored and cut into quarters
1 tomato, cut into quarters
½ lemon, cut in half
½ orange, cut into quarters
120 ml (4 fl oz/½ cup) red wine
2 litres (68 fl oz/8½ cups) tepid water
2 potatoes, peeled and roughly cut into cubes
salt and freshly ground black pepper

For the quinoa
300 g (10½ oz/1½ cups) quinoa
1 carrot, finely grated
1 celery stalk, grated
small handful of chives, snipped
1 small garlic clove, peeled and grated
1 tablespoon finely chopped parsley
salt and freshly ground black pepper
juice of ½ orange
½ teaspoon ground cinnamon

Heat the oil in a large saucepan and fry the lamb, vegetables and garlic for the stock until lightly browned. Add the herbs, spices, apple, tomato and fruit and stir through. Pour in the wine and allow it to reduce for a couple of minutes, then add the water and bring to the boil.

Reduce the heat and allow the lamb to simmer uncovered for 2–3 hours, or until soft and falling away from the bone. The cooking time will depend on the cut and size of the lamb pieces. Drop the potatoes into the pan around 20 minutes before the end of cooking time. When the potatoes are done and the lamb is tender, use a pair of tongs to lift them out of the stock and set aside to cool. Strain the broth and discard the flavourings.

Put the stock back into the pan and bring to the boil. Taste and add seasoning as necessary. Ladle out some of the broth to cook the quinoa following the instructions on the packet. Pick off the meat from the lamb bones and add to the remaining stock in the pan with the potatoes.

When the quinoa is done, stir in the other ingredients and serve still warm with the stock and lamb in a separate bowl. Guests can help themselves to the lamb, potatoes and broth as they eat the couscous.

MEAT & POULTRY

PETTINICCHIO DI MAIALE
€ 2.00
CHILO

TESTA DI MAIALE
€ 3.00
UNA

MEAT & POULTRY

Sicilians may be surrounded by water, and they certainly eat a lot of fish, but meat is still firmly on the menu when it is affordable.

Pork, particularly the black pig, is rated highly. In the past, meat was a luxury food, eaten only in the grand houses, and the poor learnt to mimic meat dishes using vegetables instead. Offal is a popular street food, particularly in the capital Palermo (see chapter one). Cheaper cuts of meat are used in the long, slow-cooking ragu on page 133 and the better cuts are often made to go further by bashing them out into escalopes, such as in the Rolled Stuffed Roast Beef on page 175.

ROAST PORK WITH APPLES & ROSEMARY

There is a breed of pig in Sicily known as Black Pig, the *suino nero*. It is small but has a good layer of fat, which ensures a succulent result to the meat. Marco Piraino, our chef friend from Palermo, showed us how he made a stunning Sunday lunch or dinner from a good cut of pork. Do try to find one from your butchers with a decent layer of fat. Even though you cut the skin away, you want enough fat under it and around the loin to keep it from drying out.

Serves 6

1.6 kg (3 lb 8 oz) pork loin on the bone
2 garlic cloves, 1 cut in half and 1 peeled and lightly crushed
salt and freshly ground black pepper
2 celery stalks, roughly chopped
1 onion, roughly chopped
2 carrots, roughly chopped
4 apples, peeled and each cut into 8 wedges
3 sprigs of rosemary
500 ml (17 fl oz/2¼ cups) white wine
1 litre (34 fl oz/4¼ cups) water, plus 100 ml (3½ fl oz/scant ½ cup)
50 g (2 oz/½ stick) salted butter

Preheat the oven to 240°C (475°F/Gas 9). Allow the pork to come to room temperature. Remove the skin from the joint, leaving a little fat on the loin and most of it on the skin. It is easy to do this yourself using a long, sharp knife, or just ask your butcher to do it for you. Score the fat with a sharp knife, such as a Stanley knife if you have one, and place in a shallow dish. Pour over half a kettle of just-boiled water – this will soften the skin and open up the pores to help the crackling (pork rinds) develop. Drain off the water and dry the skin on kitchen paper on both sides. Rub with a light sprinkling of salt. Put the skin onto an oven rack and set aside.

Rub the meat all over with the halved garlic clove, then season the joint all over. Put the remaining garlic clove with the vegetables, half of the chopped apples and 2 of the rosemary sprigs into a large, deep roasting pan and lay the meat on top. Pour in the wine and water (this can be done in two or three stages as the liquid evaporates, if your dish isn't deep enough to hold it all in one go).

Roast the pork in the oven with the skin on the rack above it so that the fat drips down on to the meat. Cook for 30 minutes then turn down the heat to 180°C (350°F/Gas 4) and continue to cook for another 1– 1½ hours or until the juices run clear when pierced in the thickest part with a skewer or the meat measures 71°C (160°F) with a probe thermometer.

When the pork is cooked, remove it from the oven and place on a serving dish to rest covered in foil and a cloth to keep warm. Let the juices in the pan settle. Remove the crackling and keep warm, but don't cover or it could become soggy. Meanwhile, cook the remaining apples in the butter with the 100 ml (3½ fl oz/ scant ½ cup) water and remaining rosemary sprig in a medium saucepan with a lid until they are just soft but not collapsed. Skim off the excess oil from the roasting pan and discard. Pour the meat juices and roasted vegetable and apple mix into a serving bowl.

Serve the pork with the buttery apples arranged around the joint and the meat juices and vegetables on the side. Enjoy with the crackling and with mashed or roast potatoes, or soft polenta, and the Purple Sprouting Broccoli on page 104.

ROTOLO DI FARSUMAGRU

ROLLED STUFFED ROAST BEEF

During the French occupation of the island, fancier ways of preparing meat were introduced. The name of this dish comes from the French words *roulé* for rolled and *farcie* for stuffed. It is a great way to use up leftovers such as ragu, spinach, roasted vegetables and cooked ham. Don't feel you have to use everything we have; you only need enough to give flavour and colour to the stuffing. The mozzarella can be swapped for provolone or a young pecorino, and the ham can be swapped for mortadella, to alter the flavour or to use what you have in the fridge. It is a popular dish as a little meat can go a long way. We love to cook this at home for a Sunday lunch or to serve for a dinner party. It looks impressive, as when cut open it reveals the colourful stuffing inside. It can be eaten hot or at room temperature.

Serves 6

---

500 g (1 lb 2 oz) lean topside of beef
salt and freshly ground black pepper
50 g (2 oz/½ stick) salted butter at
    room temperature
200 ml (7 fl oz/scant 1 cup) white wine
200 g (7 oz) Cherry Tomato Sauce
    (see page 144)
100 ml (3½ fl oz/scant ½ cup) stock
    or water
100 g (3½ oz/⅔ cup) frozen or fresh peas
small handful of rosemary sprigs, thyme
    and oregano (optional)
1 teaspoon fennel seeds

For the stuffing
200 g (7 oz) thinly cut cooked ham (about
    6 large slices)
4 eggs, hard-boiled, shelled and cut into
    1 cm (½ in) slices
400 g (14 oz) ragu (1 quantity of the Quick
    Beef Ragu, see page 131)
100 g (3½ oz/⅔ cup) cooked peas
100 g (3½ oz) Parmesan, finely grated
1 x 125 g (4 oz) ball of mozzarella,
    roughly sliced

string, for tying the meat

Preheat the oven to 200°C (400°F/Gas 6). Make a rectangle of the meat approximately 30 x 25 cm (12 x 10 in) and place on a piece of baking parchment bigger than this. To do this, cut the meat into slices around 2 cm (¾ in) thick. Trim away any obvious tough white sinew. Bash the meat out under cling film (plastic wrap) with a meat tenderiser or the flat of a small saucepan to a thickness of around 7 mm (just over ¼ in). Lay the pieces down on the parchment to make up the rectangle, overlapping them a little as necessary to form a barrier to prevent the stuffing from escaping. Season with salt and pepper. Lay the cling film over the meat again and give it a gentle bash to secure the pieces together. Discard the cling film.

First lay on the slices of cooked ham – they will help to keep your stuffing in place. Now layer on the rest of the stuffing ingredients, leaving a border of 2.5 cm (1 in) clear at one long edge. Season once more. Roll up the beef tightly starting at the long edge without the border. Secure it with string. Using your hands, slather the meat with the butter. Put the roll into a roasting tray and bake for 5 minutes. Pour over the wine and bake again for 10 minutes. Pour the tomato sauce, stock, peas and any leftover stuffing that didn't make it inside around the roll. Tuck some rosemary sprigs and oregano, if you have some, into the string and scatter over the fennel seeds.

Cook in the oven for 30–40 minutes or until cooked through. The middle should reach 60°C (140°F) using a probe thermometer, or a skewer inserted into the middle should be hot when you touch the end. Remove from the oven and serve with mashed potatoes, buttery soft polenta or brown rice and the Purple Sprouting Broccoli on page 104.

BEEF & ONIONS

This is one of my new favourite dishes. It is simple, easy to prepare and never fails to impress. The meat can be reheated in the sauce so it is good to cook it and keep it for a couple of meals during the week or prepare it the day before for a dinner party.

Serves 6

625 g (1 lb 6 oz) topside of beef
salt and freshly ground black pepper
2 tablespoons sunflower or groundnut (peanut) oil
50 g (2 oz/½ stick) salted butter
50 ml (2 fl oz/¼ cup) extra-virgin olive oil
350 g (12 oz) onions, cut in half from root
    to tip and thinly sliced into half-moons
500 ml (17 fl oz/2¼ cups) dry marsala, sherry
    or white wine

Let the beef come up to room temperature before cooking. Preheat the oven to 180°C (350°F/Gas 4). Season the beef all over then brown it in the sunflower oil in a heavy-based casserole dish. Remove the beef and set aside on a plate, discarding the oil in the pan. Add the butter and olive oil to the casserole and sweat the onions over a low heat until tender, around 10 minutes. Pour in the marsala and add the beef. Use a pair of tongs to pile the onions on top of the beef. Put the lid on the casserole and transfer to the oven for 2 hours.

Remove the beef and let it rest in a warm serving dish covered in foil and a cloth. If there is a lot of fat, this can be left to settle at this stage and scooped off. Purée the onions and cooking juices to a smooth sauce with a stick blender or leave as they are and serve with the beef. This is great with heaps of buttery mashed potatoes, soft polenta or the Sicilian Chips on page 98.

Use **3** Ways

With chicken, aubergine, veal

CHICKEN PARMIGIANA

The idea of coating flattened meat and vegetables is popular all over Italy. In the wealthier houses in Sicily, meat was pounded until just a few millimetres thick and coated with crunchy breadcrumbs and fried. The poorer households did a similar thing with aubergines (eggplants).

When large numbers of Sicilians emigrated to the US after the Second World War they took their traditional recipes with them. As they prospered abroad, they were able to replace the aubergines with chicken and the famous American–Sicilian dish of chicken parmigiana was born. Now forgive me if this recipe is a little off-track in a Sicilian cookbook, but our family happens to love this dish. For authenticity I asked Americans Pat and Diane Frustaci, of Sicilian descent, and Howard Roseman, who has knowledge of the dish, to help me out. They all live in New Jersey and work with my sister Louise. They remember their grandmothers cooking the dish, the evolution of it over the years, and were happy to help me recreate these two recipes for the book.

For a healthier choice, instead of frying the chicken, give it a light spray with olive oil and bake it in the oven until golden. Then follow the recipe as before. In America, this dish is served with buttered linguine but I prefer it with sautéed spinach, steamed greens or a salad dressed with lemon and olive oil.

Serves 4

4 skinless free-range chicken breasts (approximately 500 g/1 lb 2 oz total weight)
salt and freshly ground black pepper
2 teaspoons dried oregano, plus extra to sprinkle
50 g (2 oz/½ cup) '00', plain (all-purpose) or gluten-free flour
2 eggs, beaten
100 g (3½ oz/1 cup) dry gluten-free or wheat breadcrumbs
75 g (2½ oz) finely grated Parmesan
8–10 tablespoons seed or groundnut (peanut) oil for frying
2 garlic cloves, peeled and lightly crushed
1 quantity of Cherry Tomato Sauce (see page 144)
2 x 125 g (4 oz) balls of mozzarella, cut into 1 cm (½ in) slices and drained in a sieve
a few basil leaves, to garnish

Cut the chicken breasts in half along the side and open them up like a book. Cut through the spine of each 'book' so that you have two separate halves. Place the halves between two pieces of cling film (plastic wrap) and pound the chicken breasts with a meat tenderiser or the flat of a small saucepan until around 5 mm (¼ in) thick. Season with salt and pepper and scatter half the oregano over the flattened chicken, pressing it in with your hands. Turn the chicken breasts over and season the other side.

Preheat the oven to 200°C (400°F/Gas 6). Prepare three wide bowls, one with the flour, one with beaten egg and one with breadcrumbs mixed with half the Parmesan.

Heat a third of the oil with the garlic in a large frying pan and, when you can smell the garlic, remove the garlic from the pan and set aside. Dip the chicken breast pieces first in the flour, shaking off any excess, then in the egg and then the breadcrumbs, making sure they are evenly coated. Pan-fry until light golden brown on both sides. This should take just a couple of minutes a side. You can fry the chicken in batches, adding a little more oil and the garlic back into the pan each time, making sure the oil is hot before frying.

Pour a thin layer of the tomato sauce into a large ovenproof dish and lay over the chicken pieces. Spoon a heaped tablespoon more sauce over each piece. Arrange the mozzarella on top of the chicken and scatter over the remaining Parmesan. Bake in the oven for 10–15 minutes or until the cheese is melted and the chicken is cooked through (make sure there are no pink juices when you pierce the thickest part with a skewer or the internal temperature is 85°C (185°F) when measured with a probe thermometer). Remove from the oven and serve straight away scattered with the basil.

BREADED VEAL CUTLETS OR AUBERGINES PALERMO STYLE

The same can be done with veal or slices of aubergine: follow the instructions for the Chicken Parmigiana on page 180, but pan-fry until cooked through and eat with a squeeze of lemon rather than baking further (see the photo on page 181). The cutlets are very good with the Sweet & Sour Aubergines on page 65.

RACK OF LAMB WITH CITRUS GREMOLATA

The citrus perfume from the crust on this lamb as it cooks fills the kitchen with the scent of summer. It is quick and easy to put together and looks splendid for a quick supper or entertaining. The recipe is from Roberto Toro, Head Chef of the elegant restaurant at one of our favourite places to stay in Sicily, the hotel Belmond Grand Timeo in Taormina. Either serve the rack of lamb simply with a swirl of your best extra-virgin olive oil or make a gravy from lamb bones (this can be done the day before).

Serves 4

For the gravy
500 g (17 oz) lamb bones
1 small white or brown onion, peeled and roughly chopped
1 stick of celery and a few leaves, roughly chopped
1 carrot, roughly chopped
1 bay leaf
1 sprig rosemary
a few peppercorns
2 tablespoons extra-virgin olive oil
100 ml (3½ fl oz) white wine
3 litres cold water
2 teaspoons cornflour
10 g (¼ oz) butter
salt

2 French-trimmed 8-bone racks of lamb
salt and freshly ground black pepper
small handful of mint leaves
2 strips orange zest, peeled from an unwaxed orange with a potato peeler
2 strips lemon zest peeled from an unwaxed lemon with a potato peeler
4 teaspoons Dijon mustard
200 g (7 oz) Swiss chard leaves, stems discarded, or spinach leaves
5 tablespoons extra-virgin olive oil, plus extra to finish
1 clove garlic, peeled and lightly crushed

If you are going to make a gravy, fry the bones, onion, celery, carrot, bay leaf, rosemary and peppercorns in the oil in a large saucepan over a medium–high heat until lightly golden brown and beginning to stick to the bottom of the pan. Pour in the wine and allow it to sizzle for a few minutes. Add the water and bring to the boil. Turn the heat down to simmer and leave the stock to bubble away for 2–3 hours. Strain the stock through a colander and discard the flavourings. Put the stock back into the pan over a medium heat and reduce it further until you have around 500ml (17 fl oz). In a small cup, stir 4 tablespoons of the stock with the cornflour until it forms a smooth paste. Whisk into the stock with the butter and season to taste. The gravy is now ready to use straight away or can be cooled and stored in the fridge until you need it. When ready to serve, reheat in a small pan.

To cook the rack of lamb, heat the oven to 180°C (350°F/Gas 4). Split the racks into two. Season the lamb all over and briefly sauté on all sides in a large frying pan (skillet) with 2 tablespoons of the extra-virgin olive oil.

Finely chop the mint, lemon and orange zest together on a board. Spread it out into a thin layer.

Spread each rack of lamb with a little mustard and dip it into the chopped orange, lemon and mint to coat. Place onto a baking tray and cook in the oven for 12 minutes – it will be pink on the inside.

In the meantime, boil the chard or spinach leaves for a few minutes in salted water. Drain well and squeeze the excess water away. Sauté with the garlic in the remaining oil. Put the chard leaves on the plate and lay the rack of lamb on top. Finish with a swirl of your best extra-virgin olive oil or the lamb gravy.

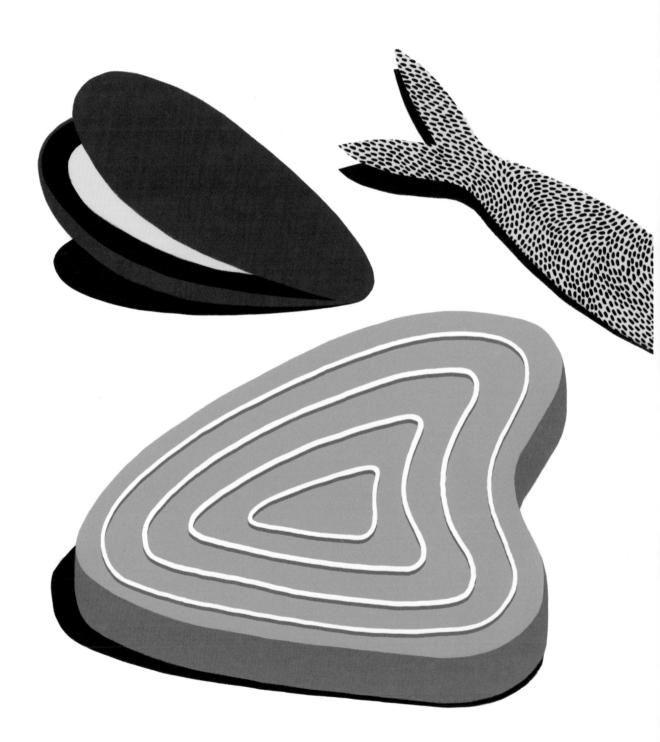

FISH

FISH

From our room in the Palladio hotel in Giardini Naxos we watched the sun rise and the fishing boats gather in the harbour, obviously preparing to follow one another to an area where a shoal had been found. Later in the morning we went to the market with Caterina, the hotel owner, and saw the fish being brought in from the boats. We bought swordfish, tuna and sardines and returned to the hotel to cook them with her. 'It's all about the freshness and provenance,' she said.

The most popular fish in Sicily are tuna and swordfish and you will find them on menus raw, cooked and smoked, all delicious. There are plenty of other varieties, referred to as blue for oily fish, red for fish such as tuna and white for the rest.

In Palermo, you can go to the Borgo Vecchio and watch the locals choose their fish from the fishmonger's stand and take it to Da Michele, where it will be cooked right there and then. At the port you can see fishmongers waiting with their marble slabs and sharp knives at the ready. As soon as the boats come in, they are all set to start scaling, cleaning and filleting the fish ready to sell.

There are wonderful seafood restaurants, like Sakalleo in Scoglitti, which have no menu but instead serve a stream of the freshest seafood until you can eat no more and say, 'Stop!'

When we were there, a group of Sicilian men descended on the restaurant Apollonion in Ortigia and clearly relished their food. They were obviously regulars and knew the owner Carlo well. He was also the chef and ducked in and out of the kitchen, bringing out enormous platters of shellfish, mussels, fish in *caponata* and tuna to the men. He also found time to cuddle his granddaughter (who will apparently take over the restaurant one day) and clear plates all at the same time. The men crushed the skeletons of the crustaceans with their hands and sucked out the insides, mopping up the juices with bread soaked in oil, oregano and chilli and quaffing short tumblers of Nero d'Avola. They were all chefs and had just finished cooking pizza at a culinary fair and were enjoying a day off. 'When we eat, we are serious,' one said to us as dish after dish came out to satisfy their furious appetites. What a wonderful way to spend your day off, I thought.

SALMON BAKED WITH ORANGES & THYME

Oranges of various types are available most of the year round in Sicily but the most popular, the blood orange Tarocco, can only be found in the winter months. Salmon stands up well to the sweet flavour of orange and, married with the thyme and pepper, this incredibly simple dish becomes more impressive than the sum of its parts.

Serves 4

2 sweet oranges
4 salmon fillets (approximately 700 g/
    1 lb 9 oz total weight)
a few sprigs of thyme, leaves stripped
salt and freshly ground black pepper
2 tablespoons extra-virgin olive oil
100 ml (3½ fl oz/scant ½ cup) white wine

Preheat the oven to 180°C (350°F/Gas 4). Cut away the skin and all the white pith from the oranges. Neatly cut the segments from between the membrane and set aside, collecting any juice in a bowl. Make four cuts into the salmon fillets at a 45 degree angle, stopping 1 cm (½ in) short of the skin. Insert an orange segment into each cut and put the fillets (skin side down) into an ovenproof dish. Scatter over the thyme leaves and season the fish with salt and plenty of pepper. Pour over the reserved orange juice, olive oil and wine. Scatter any remaining segments of orange around the fish. Bake for 20 minutes or until the fish is firm to the touch and cooked through. Serve hot with the Purple Sprouting Broccoli on page 104 or the Couscous Salad on page 106.

SAUTÉED MUSSELS IN GARLIC & WHITE WINE

Much of the west of the island is uninhabited; it is raw and wild, with random deserted towns, stunning beaches and pretty countryside. In the middle of nowhere is the village of Cozze, meaning mussels, presumably where they grew naturally.

The isolated Cozzara restaurant just outside the village is a magnet for the locals, who come from miles around to eat steaming bowls of the freshest mussels you are likely to taste. There was what seemed to be a bottomless bowl of the most delicious seafood, and charred yellow *semola* toast to soak up the incredible fish juices in the soup. We used one mussel shell to pick at the plump pinky-orange morsels inside the rest. Tanks of seawater outside keep the fish fresh until just before they are cooked. A huge tank full of lobsters was down to its last by the end of the night. Now I know why people drive miles just to get here. It is an eating experience like no other.

Serves 4

---

3 tablespoons extra-virgin olive oil
3 garlic cloves, peeled and thinly sliced
salt and freshly ground black pepper
1 kg (2 lb 3 oz) fresh live mussels, cleaned
    and debearded
100 ml (3½ fl oz/scant ½ cup) white wine
large handful of parsley, finely chopped

Heat the oil with the garlic and some seasoning in a large frying pan with a lid. When you can smell the garlic, add the mussels and wine. Cover and cook, shaking the pan frequently. When the last mussel opens (discard any that stay shut), add the parsley and serve straight away with the Sicilian Focaccia on page 37.

TUNA STEAKS IN A QUINOA CRUST ON COURGETTES

This light and lovely dish comes from the stunning Belmond Grand Hotel Timeo in Taormina. The method of cooking the tuna in a crust in the oven means that it is a fantastic dish for entertaining, and we love the contrast of the buttery, crunchy coating and the pink rare tuna inside. It is also gluten-free. A quicker version if you are in a hurry is to coat the fish in finely crushed pistachios instead. The courgette (zucchini) batons are so easy to make they have become a staple vegetable in our house. I have even had them for breakfast with scrambled eggs.

**Serves 4 as a main course
or 6 as a starter**

---

100 g (3½ oz/½ cup) quinoa
280 ml (9¾ fl oz/scant 1¼ cups) water
salt and freshly ground black pepper
25 g (1 oz/2 tablespoons) salted butter
100 ml (3½ fl oz/scant ½ cup) freshly
   squeezed orange juice
50 g (2 oz/scant ¼ cup) caster (superfine)
   sugar
80 ml (2¾ fl oz/⅓ cup) white wine vinegar
6 cardamom pods, lightly crushed to
   open them
1 star anise
1 teaspoon black peppercorns
600 g (1 lb 5 oz) sustainably caught fresh
   tuna, cut into 4 or 6 steaks
1 egg white, loosely beaten
2 courgettes (zucchini), cut into
   julienne strips
2 tablespoons extra-virgin olive oil
sea salt flakes
a few micro leaves or mint, to garnish

Preheat the oven to 180°C (350°F/Gas 4). Cook the quinoa in the water with a pinch of salt until the liquid evaporates completely. Keep stirring the pan with a wooden spoon; the quinoa will crackle and won't cook through but you will have a lovely crunchy result. Melt the butter in a frying pan and add the dried-out quinoa. Sauté the quinoa until it turns golden brown – around 5 minutes should do it. Transfer to a large plate and allow to cool.

Mix the orange juice, sugar and vinegar together in a saucepan and bring to the boil, then reduce the heat and let the sauce bubble for 5 minutes. Remove from the heat and add the spices. Let them infuse for 20 minutes and then strain the sauce through a sieve into a bowl.

Season the tuna steaks with salt. Dip them in the egg white and then in the crispy quinoa and bake in an ovenproof dish for 6 minutes. Meanwhile, sauté the courgettes in the oil with a little seasoning for just a couple of minutes and place some in the centre of each plate. Cut the tuna steaks in half, put them on the zucchini and drizzle over a little of the spiced orange sauce, with a few splashes around the plate. Serve straight away garnished with some sea salt flakes and a few micro or mint leaves.

Variation: Coat the tuna steaks in 50 g (2 oz) peeled green pistachios roughly ground in a food processor instead of the quinoa.

SWORDFISH WITH SALMORIGLIO SAUCE

This sauce works well on more or less all types of fish: try grilled (broiled) prawns (shrimp), sea bream fillets, roasted whole sea bass or tuna steaks. It is good on grilled chicken and lamb, too. We have also included it in the vegetable chapter, to use on courgette (zucchini) ribbons, but the process is a little different for fish.

Serves 4

---

4 swordfish steaks
extra-virgin olive oil

For the *salmoriglio* dressing
2 tablespoons parsley, finely chopped
1 small garlic clove, peeled and
  finely chopped
1 heaped teaspoon fresh or dried oregano
4 tablespoons extra-virgin olive oil
2 tablespoons lemon juice
salt and freshly ground black pepper

To make the dressing, put the parsley and garlic together in a bowl, pour over 3 tablespoons of boiling water and add the oregano. Use the back of a spoon to press the herbs and garlic down in the water – this helps to release the essential oils and adds to the flavour. Pour in the oil and set aside to cool. Add the lemon juice and season to taste.

Marinate the fish in half the dressing for 30 minutes, but no longer than 1 hour or it will start to 'cook' in the acidity of the lemon. Grill (broil), barbecue or cook in a griddle pan with a little olive oil for 1–2 minutes on each side or until just cooked. If you can, turn the fish 180 degrees midway through so that it has an attractive crosshatch pattern on the outside. Serve with the remaining dressing on the side and with the Couscous Salad on page 106 or the Orange & Fennel Salad on page 111.

DRUNKEN TUNA WITH SWEET & SOUR ONIONS

A full-bodied red wine such as the Sicilian Nero d'Avola is ideal for this recipe from Gregorio Piazza, our Sicilian head chef from our restaurant Caldesi in Campagna. The sauce can be left as just that, a sauce. Alternatively, it can be reduced further to the sticky stage of a relish, which makes it ideal to eat with cheese, sausages or the Sardine Patties on page 50. Both the sauce and the relish can be stored in the fridge for up to a week.

Serves 4–6

---

3 red onions, cut in half from root to tip
    and sliced into 5 mm (¼ in) half-moons
1 garlic clove, peeled and roughly sliced
6 tablespoons extra-virgin olive oil
salt and freshly ground black pepper
25 g (1 oz/scant ¼ cup) sultanas
    (golden raisins)
50 g (2 oz/scant ¼ cup) caster (superfine)
    sugar
400 ml (13 fl oz/1¾ cups) red wine, such
    as Nero d'Avola
600 g (1 lb 5 oz) sustainably caught
    fresh tuna, cut into 4–6 steaks
25 g (1 oz/2 tablespoons) salted butter
a little parsley, finely chopped

Put the onions and garlic into a large non-stick frying pan with 4 tablespoons of the oil and some seasoning. Sweat them gently for 30 minutes, or until really soft and dark in colour. Add the sultanas, sugar and half the wine and cook slowly for 10–15 minutes to reduce the wine. Stop when the reduction has the consistency of a sauce (or reduce further to a relish).

Season the tuna with salt and pepper and fry in the remaining oil in a pan for about 2 minutes each side. Pour in the remaining wine and let it bubble and reduce for a couple of minutes. Tip the pan to one side to collect the sauce and spoon it over the fish. Add a good spoonful of the onions to the pan and top with a knob of butter. Shake the pan to combine. You might not be able to do this all in one go, in which case cook two steaks at a time, each with a little of the wine and butter, and leave on a warm plate while you cook the rest. Serve the tuna with the onions on top and garnished with a little parsley. This is good with the Sicilian Chips on page 98, mashed potato or sautéed spinach.

Use **3** Ways

With meat, fish, cheese

GRIDDLED MACKEREL WITH CAPONATA

Originally *caponata* was always made with fish but in the hands of the poor, who couldn't afford fish, aubergines (eggplants) were used instead. Nowadays, it is eaten with both. It can be made a couple of days in advance and kept in the fridge. In fact, the flavour of *caponata* is always better a day or two after it's made, but be sure to bring it to room temperature before using.

We use our griddle pan for cooking the fish as I like the visual effect of the black lines on the fish and the fact that the fat drains away into the grooves of the pan. However, a hot grill in the oven or a rack over a barbecue work just as well. Sardines or sea bass or bream are ideal cooked in this way too, and the jewel-like sweet and sour *caponata* is the perfect foil for all types of fish.

Serves 4

---

4 mackerel fillets
1 tablespoon extra-virgin olive oil
salt and freshly ground black pepper
1 quantity of *caponata* (see page 65)
handful of parsley, roughly chopped

Put a griddle pan over a medium heat to get it hot. Brush the mackerel fillets with olive oil on both sides and season with salt and pepper. Place the fillets skin-side down on the hot griddle pan and cook for around 3 minutes until the skin is crispy. Turn and cook the fillets on the other side for 2 minutes or until cooked through. Remove from the pan with a fish slice and lay on warm serving plates. Serve with the *caponata* on the side and scattered with parsley. The Sicilian Chips on page 98 or a simple green salad go well with this dish.

STUFFED SARDINES WITH SPINACH, PINE NUTS & RAISINS

Originally, this dish was made with small birds. Translated literally, *beccafico* means 'fig-peckers'. You will find various forms of this traditional Sicilian dish all over the island. This is Gregorio Piazza's way of cooking it; he comes from Augusta, to the east of Sicily, where they use spinach and oranges.

Serves 6

500 g (1 lb 2 oz) spinach
7 tablespoons extra-virgin olive oil
1 garlic clove, peeled and roughly sliced
salt and freshly ground black pepper
50 g (2 oz/⅓ cup) pine nuts
50 g (2 oz/⅓ cup) sultanas (golden raisins),
    soaked in warm water for 30 minutes
40 g (1½ oz/½ cup) fresh breadcrumbs, made from
    the inside of a crusty loaf (can be gluten-free)
12 fresh sardines, heads removed and filleted
    (360 g/12½ oz after cleaning)
1 orange, sliced
8 bay leaves

12 cocktail sticks

Steam the spinach briefly until soft. Drain and allow to cool. Squeeze out the water so that you have a dryish ball of spinach. Chop it finely on a board. Heat 3 tablespoons of the oil in a large frying pan and fry the garlic for just a minute over a medium heat. Add the spinach to the pan and season. Use a wooden spoon to stir it around.

Put the pine nuts and sultanas on a board and roughly chop them together, then add to the pan with the spinach and stir through. Cook for around 5 minutes, stirring continuously. Remove from the heat and allow to cool. Mix with the breadcrumbs in a bowl.

Preheat the oven to 170°C (325°F/Gas 3) and grease an ovenproof dish with 1 tablespoon of the oil. Lay the sardine fillets on a chopping board, season lightly with salt and pepper and drizzle 1 tablespoon of the oil over them. Place a sardine in the palm of your hand, lay a line of stuffing down the spine, roll up the fish and secure with a cocktail stick. Repeat with the rest of the sardines and put them all into the dish. Put the orange slices and bay leaves between the fish. Drizzle over the remaining olive oil and bake in the oven for 20–25 minutes. Serve warm or at room temperature with antipasti, or as a main course with salad or rice.

SEA BASS BAKED IN A PARCEL WITH SFINCIONE SAUCE

This simple recipe can be made with most white fish, such as sea bream, cod, halibut or hake. The *sfincione* sauce on page 35 is really versatile and in this recipe it is used as a base for steamed white fish in a parcel. Cooking 'al cartoccio', in a parcel, is one of my favourite ways to cook fish. When our boys were growing up I used to get them to make up their own parcels, adding their favourite ingredients to the fish inside, such as cherry tomatoes, parsley or finely sliced courgettes (zucchini). Then they would write their names on the outside of the parcel to claim ownership!

Serves 4

---

300 g (10½ oz) *sfincione* sauce
  (see page 35)
4 sea bass or sea bream fillets
8 teaspoons extra-virgin olive oil
salt and freshly ground black pepper
4 sprigs of flat-leaf parsley
120 ml (4 fl oz/½ cup) white wine

Preheat the oven to 200°C (400°F/Gas 6). Spread 4 sheets of baking parchment out on a work surface and spoon on 4 even portions of the sauce. Lay over the fillets, drizzle a couple of teaspoons of olive oil over each one and season with salt and pepper. Place a parsley sprig on each fillet, then wrap up the parcels like presents by pulling the parchment up from the front and back to the centre. Fold the top edges together over and over again, leaving the join in the centre, then turn the side ends inwards several times to seal in the juices. Place the parcels on a baking tray and put into the oven for 12–15 minutes. Feel the fish from the outside of the bag to make sure it is firm to the touch. Remove, unwrap the centre join carefully to let out the steam and bring to the table still *al cartoccio*. Serve with heaps of courgettes (zucchini) from the tuna recipe on page 196.

SWORDFISH WITH TOMATOES, CAPERS & OLIVES

Caterina, passionate foodie and owner of the charming Palladio hotel in Giardini Naxos, took us on a trip to the local fish market. She showed us a huge swordfish being filleted and told us to use a belly cut or other fatty area of the fish for this recipe. However, if you can't find this cut I have used the standard swordfish steaks you find in most supermarkets with a fish counter and it is still delicious. *Alla ghiotta*, meaning 'glutton-style', is a speciality of the Messina area in the north-east of the island.

Serves 4

1 white onion, finely chopped
1 celery stalk, finely sliced
4 tablespoons extra-virgin olive oil
100 g (3½ oz) fresh tomatoes, diced, or cherry tomatoes, cut in half
a little red chilli, finely chopped
2 tablespoons raisins
2 tablespoons pine nuts
small handful of green olives, stoned and split in two
2 tablespoons salted capers, soaked and drained
100 g (3½ oz/generous ⅓ cup) tinned chopped tomatoes
600 g (1 lb 5 oz) swordfish, cut into 4 steaks
salt and freshly ground black pepper

Cook the onion and celery in the oil with 4 tablespoons of water over a low heat until very soft – this will take 10–15 minutes. Turn the heat up a little and add the fresh tomatoes, chilli, raisins and pine nuts. Cover and cook for 5 minutes, then add the olives, capers and tinned tomatoes and cover again. Add the fish after about 5 minutes, when the tomatoes have broken down. Leave to simmer, covered, for 15–20 minutes until the fish is cooked through and the sauce has concentrated. Check the seasoning and serve with fresh crusty bread.

DOLCI & COCKTAILS

DoLCI

Sicily is known to be one of the best places in the world for its dazzling array of sweet delights – patisserie, *gelati, granite, marzipan, cannoli* and *cassata*, to name just a few. With its bounty of citrus fruits, wonderful sheep's milk ricotta, almonds and pistachios, as well as the Arab influence and the once thriving sugar industry, it is no surprise that Sicily is the place to go if you have a sweet tooth.

It was the Arabs who first mixed the snow from Mount Etna with fruit-flavoured syrups to produce *sherbets*, which were later turned into *granite*. They made marzipan cubes from water, almonds, honey and *gela*, a firm jelly made from the juice of watermelons and cinnamon. They also introduced the flavours of jasmine, orange water and rose, still popular today, and they sweetened ricotta with sugar and added spice, which began the history of the *cassata* and *cannoli*. I haven't included either *cassata* or *cannoli* here as I feel they are pastries that really only work in Sicily. The sheep's ricotta, which is so hard to find in the UK, is what gives the pleasant tang to the desserts and helps to balance the incredible sweetness.

The Spanish brought cocoa beans into Modica from Mexico and at the well-known chocolate shop Dolceria Bonajuto chocolate is produced using the same techniques as centuries ago. They use cocoa mass as it is, with no added cocoa butter or soy lecithin. It goes into a double boiler at 40°C (104°F), which doesn't melt the sugar. The grainy texture is an acquired taste. It isn't important to them that the sugar melts – the important thing is that the cocoa has 100 per cent flavour.

The traditional flavourings have always been vanilla and cinnamon and the best quality you can get. The staff will tell you that the cocoa changes the flavour of the spice, not the other way around. They run tours so that you can see the chocolatiers shaking the tins during the *battitura* as the chocolate cools. The chocolate was originally used in a drink, which they still make every Christmas. They also produce a delicious liqueur which is a tribute to the Maya tradition of mixing chocolate and chilli. Do pick up a bottle when visiting – it is wonderful on a cold night.

The famous patisserie Casatelle at Erice should probably come with a health warning. The sweets behind the counter are perfectly beautiful and totally irresistible. If you are cutting down on sugar, beware the temptations in Sicily!

ALMONDS

The sweet smell of the almond blossom is wonderful in spring and it is a great time to visit the island. Ground almonds are widely used in Sicilian cooking: they are ground into cakes, used to make milk, ice cream and *granite*, as well as chopped and added to salads, couscous and aubergine (eggplant) dishes.

Use 3 Ways

To drink,
for granita (see
page 219), for
biscuits

ALMOND MILK

This recipe is based on the one from our book *Venice: Recipes Lost and Found*. Almond milk has been made since medieval times in Europe and was thought to have restorative properties. It was useful as you could make it as you needed it, rather than cow's milk, which would have required refrigeration. This same method can be followed to make hazelnut milk. Use the nut milk for the Almond Granita on page 219, the Almond Milk Puddings on page 252 or simply to drink. This recipe will give you a distinctive almond flavour and thickish milk. If you don't want the bits or you want a thinner milk, you can strain it and add more water, but I like to keep them in. If you do strain it, dry the almond meal out in a low oven and, when completely dry, store in an airtight container. Use it whenever ground almonds are called for, particularly in the Almond & Pecorino Biscuits on page 258.

To make almond milk, place 100 g (3½ oz/⅔ cup) shelled but not peeled almonds in enough cold water to cover them and soak overnight; change the water once during this time. Strain, discard the water and put the nuts into a food processor. Blend them with 400 ml (13 fl oz/1¾ cups) of filtered water until finely ground. Pour into a large lidded jug or bowl, cover and store in the fridge for up to 3 days.

MARZIPAN

From almonds we move on to marzipan, which is called *pasta reale*, 'royal paste', in Sicily. A mixture of sugar, almonds and egg whites, marzipan can be sculpted into shapes and sets firm while maintaining a soft interior. We were struck by the wonderful marzipan sweets on sale in Peccatucci di Mamma Andrea, Piazza Ignazio Florio in Palermo, where rows of plump globes of chocolate, lemon, orange or pistachio marzipan line up for you to pop into your mouth. They are not too sweet and have none of the synthetic flavours that seem to put people off marzipan. I never liked it as a child but now I have learnt to make it, I have finally caught the bug.

Apparently, when an important bishop came to visit the Martorana convent attached to the church of Santa Maria dell'Ammiraglio in Palermo, the nuns shaped fruits from marzipan and hung them in the trees. Since then marzipan fruits have been called *frutta di Martorana*, and to this day children receive them on All Souls' Day, the equivalent of our Halloween.

Makes approximately
1 kg (2 lb 3 oz)

---

160 ml (5½ fl oz/⅔ cup) water
1 tablespoon liquid glucose
1 teaspoon almond extract
500 g (1 lb 2 oz/4 cups) icing
    (confectioner's) sugar
500 g (1 lb 2 oz/5 cups) ground almonds
flavourings of your choice, to taste
    (optional)

Put the water into a saucepan and bring to the boil. Add the glucose and stir through with a wooden spoon. Add the almond extract and the sugar and stir again. Keep over a low heat and add the ground almonds a little at a time, stirring continuously, until fully combined and formed into a ball of dough. Remove from the saucepan and put onto a clean worktop. If the marizpan is sticky, dust the work surface and your hands with a little icing sugar.

At this point you can knead in the flavourings of your choice, such as finely grated citrus zest or rosewater – or any others that spring to mind! Add them according to taste.

Next, roll the marzipan into little balls and either keep them as they are or form into shapes. Leave them to dry slightly overnight at room temperature. They will keep for up to a month in a sealed container.

SOFT ALMOND BISCUITS

These biscuits have been favourites of ours since our earliest visits to Sicily almost 20 years ago. Little did we know that they would become a staple in our house when we found out Giancarlo couldn't eat gluten any more. The biscuits can be flavoured with the addition of a little lemon or orange zest.

Makes 15–18 biscuits

---

150 g (5 oz/scant 1½ cups)
   ground almonds
75 g (2½ oz/scant ⅔ cup) icing
   (confectioner's) sugar
1 tablespoon runny honey
1 teaspoon almond extract
25 ml (1 fl oz) egg white
   (approximately 1 medium egg)

To decorate or flavour
jam of your choice
walnuts or almonds

Preheat the oven to 180°C (350°F/Gas 4) and line a baking tray with baking parchment. Mix together the ground almonds and icing sugar. Add the honey, almond extract and egg white and mix until you have a smooth paste. Roll the paste into small balls, approximately 3 cm (1¼ in) wide, and press the centre down lightly with your thumb to make a small well. Place the biscuits on the baking tray, pour ½ teaspoon of your favourite jam into the centre of each one or press a nut into the well. Bake in the oven for 10–12 minutes or until lightly golden. Remove from the oven and transfer to a wire rack to cool. Keep in an airtight container for up to a week, although they will harden with time.

CLEMENTINE & ALMOND SLICE

We first saw these deliciously bittersweet biscuits (see the photo on page 246) when we had tea at the house of our friends Giuseppe and Chetina while they talked to us about Sicily's rich culinary history. They had huge old jars which were used to preserve fruit through winter and they introduced me to the Clementine Marmalade on page 249. I loved it inside the pastry. The marmalade is low-sugar, so if you are using shop-bought do find one that is similar or it will be too sweet for the cake.

Serves 10–12

---

unsalted butter, for greasing
280 g (10 oz/scant cup) low-sugar orange marmalade or homemade Clementine Marmalade (see page 249)
2 teaspoons icing (confectioner's) sugar
100 g (3½ oz/generous 1 cup) flaked almonds

Shortcrust pastry
100 g (3½ oz/generous ¾ cup) icing (confectioner's) sugar
2 egg yolks
finely grated zest of ½ orange or 1 clementine
250 g (9 oz/2 cups) '00' flour, plus extra for dusting
125 g (4 oz/½ cup) chilled salted butter

Make the pastry by mixing all the ingredients together briefly in a food processor. Try to touch the pastry as little as possible. Cover with cling film (plastic wrap) and rest in the fridge for at least 1 hour or overnight.

Preheat the oven to 170°C (325°F/Gas 3) and grease a 36 x 13 cm (14¼ x 5 in) (or similar size) loose-bottomed shallow, fluted tart tin with a generous coating of butter. Roll out the chilled pastry on a well-floured surface to a thickness of about 5 mm (¼ in). Roll onto the rolling pin and transfer to the tart tin. Push the pastry well into the corners and mend any holes. Trim round the edge of the tin and gather the remaining pastry together into a ball. Cover with cling film and put in the fridge. Meanwhile, pour a layer of marmalade over the pastry in the tin.

Remove the pastry ball from the fridge, unwrap it, and coarsely grate it over the marmalade. Mix the icing sugar and almonds together in a bowl and scatter evenly over the top. Bake in the oven for 30 minutes or until the almonds are lightly caramelised. Allow to cool before removing from the tin and cutting into slices.

GRANITE

The texture of granita changes from one café or kiosk to another – it can be smooth and slushy or rougher and grainier to eat. A version seen in Sicily and Rome is grated ice with various fruit syrups of your choice poured over. Hundreds of years in between but remarkably similar to the Arab *sherbets* from centuries before.

ALMOND GRANITA

Sitting between the orange baroque buildings in the stunning town of Noto we delighted in sampling the local almond granita. Just as well it was served in small glasses, as it was incredibly sweet, but it was lovely to feel the tiny ice crystals melt on your tongue. I have cut the sugar right back in this recipe but do add more if you have a sweet tooth.

Serves 4 in shot glasses

---

1 tablespoon icing (confectioner's) sugar
200 ml (7 fl oz/scant 1 cup) homemade
  Almond Milk (see page 211)

Stir the sugar into the milk in a shallow freezer-proof container and freeze for 1 hour. Use a fork to scrape the mixture from the edges of the container into the creamy centre. Freeze again for 30 minutes and do the same again. Repeat until the granita has completely frozen into a sandy texture of ice crystals. You can either leave it grainy like this or put it into a food processor and briefly blitz to reduce it to a velvety smooth consistency instead. Serve straight away in chilled shot glasses with teaspoons.

COFFEE GRANITA

Swap the almond milk for black filter coffee and sweeten to taste. Freeze as on page 219. To be very Sicilian, slap a scoop of this between a brioche bun and add whipped cream. This is a Sicilian breakfast – wow!

RASPBERRY GRANITA

You will very often see mulberry granita on offer in Sicily but as mulberries are hard to find here in the UK we have made a raspberry version instead. It is refreshing served over a simple fresh fruit salad or as a wonderful palate cleanser between courses. Any leftover granita can be spooned into ice-cold flute glasses and topped up with Prosecco or champagne for a decadent treat.

Serves 4 in shot glasses

Blend the ingredients together in a food processor and freeze as on page 219.

400 g (14 oz/3¼ cups) raspberries
120 ml (4 fl oz/½ cup) water
4 tablespoons icing (confectioner's)
   sugar

SICILIAN ICE CREAM

Look in any guidebook and it will tell you not to miss the experience of eating ice cream in Sicily. In the lower main square outside the Duomo di San Giorgio in Ragusa Ibla is the specialist ice-cream shop Gelati di Vini. Do pay a visit and sit outside in the square while you eat ice cream and admire the pastel-coloured houses – obviously painted to match the flavours in the shop, we thought. We met a lovely English couple who didn't mind us dipping into their ices, and between us we tasted rose, jasmine, fichi d'India, Moscato, Mayan specialities with chocolate and spices, cinnamon and chilli, toasted almond packed with nuts, olive oil flavour and even a deep purple beetroot. These are proper artisanal ice creams made with love and care.

THE ICE-CREAM BASE

This base has been extensively researched and developed by our good friend and ice-cream *appassionato* Steve Adams. Personally, I think it was all a ruse simply to eat more of the stuff, but I have to say it is the best *gelato* I have ever tasted. He puts it all down to resting the base in the fridge for up to three days; it is smoother, thicker and has a velvety consistency as you eat it.

Serves 8 (makes approximately 800 ml/28 fl oz)

---

500 ml (17 fl oz/2¼ cups) whole milk
200 ml (7 fl oz/scant 1 cup) double (heavy) cream
125 g (4 oz/generous ½ cup) caster (superfine) sugar
6 egg yolks

In a large saucepan, heat the milk and cream together over a medium heat until just bubbling. Meanwhile, in a large bowl beat together the eggs and sugar until smooth. Add 2 ladlefuls of hot milk to the egg mixture and immediately whisk together. Pour this back into the pan and whisk everything together until thickened.

To sterilise the ice cream, turn up the heat and increase the temperature of the mixture to 85°C (185°F), stirring constantly. If you don't have a thermometer, this is the point when the ice cream coats the back of a spoon. Take off the heat immediately and pour into a large heatproof bowl. To cool quickly, set this bowl over another bowl full of iced water, and then cover the surface of the custard with cling film (plastic wrap) to stop a skin from forming. Stir every so often to help it cool evenly. When cool, pass the custard through a fine sieve. The custard can be made into ice cream straight away, or, like Steve, you can rest it for up to 3 days in the fridge for a fuller flavour and velvety texture. Churn in an ice-cream machine or by hand using the method below.

Making ice cream without an ice-cream machine
If you don't have an ice-cream machine, when the custard is cool, pass it through a sieve into a shallow, freezer-proof container and put it into the freezer. Whisk the mixture every hour for 4 hours to break down the ice crystals as they form. When it has all frozen it is ready to eat, or cover and leave for another day. An alternative method is to freeze the mixture in ice cube trays or small yoghurt pots and, when frozen, tip the contents into a food processor and blend to break up the ice crystals. Cover and freeze again straight away before it has a chance to melt. This is the quickest and easiest way to do it, and it results in a smooth gelato, but you do need space in your freezer and a sturdy food processor.

ROSE

We tried spritzing some of our Welsh rosewater, Petals from the Valley, directly on to the frozen ice cream just before serving. It is wonderful and makes you feel like someone has just given you a bouquet of roses, told you they love you and asked you to marry them! However, if you don't have a spray to hand add approximately 3–4 tablespoons of rosewater (depending on your taste and brand of rosewater) to the hot custard. Taste and adjust accordingly.

VANILLA

Sitting on this terrace at Sant'Andrea hotel in Taormina eating cool vanilla ice cream in the hot sun was heavenly. Add the seeds of a vanilla pod to the custard base while it is still hot. Leave the pod in the mixture too until you are ready to churn.

CHOCOLATE & CINNAMON

This is a flavour inspired by the amusing and unusual Dolceria Bonajuto chocolate shop in Modica, where they sell a Mayan-inspired liqueur made from chocolate and spices. Add 200 g (7 oz) dark (bittersweet) chocolate (minimum 70% cocoa solids), broken into small pieces, into the hot custard, off the heat, as soon as it thickens, with 2 teaspoons ground cinnamon and a pinch of salt. Taste and adjust the salt and cinnamon flavours as necessary. For a kick of heat, add a dried red chilli to the milk and cream as they heat. Remove before freezing.

SAFFRON

Saffron strands will vary in flavour depending on their age and quality. To make this, we use 3 level teaspoons of saffron strands. Add to the base while it is still hot, according to taste – you may find you need more or less than our measurement. Do bear in mind that you need a fairly robust flavour as the strength softens when it is frozen.

CLEMENTINE

We love the subtle flavour of clementines but you could use any citrus fruit to flavour the ice cream as follows: add 2 teaspoons of finely grated clementine zest to the hot custard base.

VANILLA OLIVE OIL

This brilliantly simple idea comes from the restaurant in Palermo called Bio and Sicily. 'Bio' means organic and the restaurant specialises in zero-kilometre food that is grown organically. In this case, they have used a local light oil and in the words of the manager, Marco Piraino, 'mixed it with vanilla pods and time'.

We make small amounts as, although it keeps well in a small bottle, a little olive oil on a dessert goes a long way. Simply put around 50 ml (2 fl oz/ ¼ cup) of a delicate light extra-virgin olive oil in a jar and mix with the seeds of a vanilla pod and the bean cut into a few pieces so that it fits in the jar. Screw on the lid and leave in a cool, dark place for at least 3 days and up to 10 days. The flavour will develop with time. When you are ready to use it, shake the bottle to distribute the vanilla seeds and drizzle over ice cream, whipped cream and berries or fresh fruit salad.

Use 3 Ways

Strawberries and cream, ice cream, fruit salad

CAROB BISCUITS

Carob trees are plentiful in Sicily. Historically, they provided shade for cattle and the beans became fodder for the animals. In hard times carob beans were ground into flour, which is naturally sweet and has a lovely caramel flavour; it was used to replace coffee in drinks and precious chocolate, luxuries out of the reach of Sicily's poor. I have also heard of carob gnocchi.

I buy huge bags of almonds as I love the milk they produce. They are cheaper and I believe better for you when they are still brown and in their thin skins but the recipe will work if you only have blanched almonds. I use the leftover almond meal from making Almond Milk (see page 211), and soft Medjool dates as I like their natural sweetness, but if you prefer you can add sugar instead.

Makes approximately 20 biscuits

---

200 g (7 oz/1⅓ cups) almonds
100 g (3½ oz/scant 1 cup) carob flour
3 egg whites
100 g (3½ oz/scant ½ cup) salted butter
6 Medjool dates, stoned, or 1 tablespoon
   caster (superfine) sugar

Preheat the oven to 180°C (350°F/Gas 4) and line a baking tray with baking parchment. Put the almonds into a food processor and grind to a sandy texture. Add the remaining ingredients and blend again to combine. You should end up with a soft and sticky dough.

Wet your hands with water and roll walnut-sized balls of dough. Lay them on the prepared tray, spaced apart by at least 5 cm (2 in). Flatten them slightly with the back of a damp fork or spoon and bake in the oven for 8–10 minutes, or until the biscuits start to crack and become firm to the touch.

Variations: Add the seeds of 4 cardamom pods or 2 teaspoons of ground cinnamon to the mix for a wonderfully spiced flavour.

MARSALA SEMIFREDDO WITH CARAMELISED NUTS & RED WINE REDUCTION

On the hilltop above Cefalù in the tiny village of Sant'Ambrogio you will find a gem of a restaurant owned by the Zito family. Mimmo, the owner and chef, let me try his latest invention of wild fennel *semifreddo*. I'm afraid you will have to take my word for the fact it was wonderful – sadly, I was unable to extract the recipe from him as he had just made it up that morning and had no quantities to give me! Instead, we also loved the creamy marsala *semifreddo* below, with its surprise of caramelised nuts inside and its indulgent, warm red wine sauce.

Serves 8–10

For the *semifreddo*
3 eggs, separated
400 ml (13 fl oz/1¾ cups) whipping cream
1 teaspoon vanilla extract
150 g (5 oz/⅔ cup) caster (superfine) sugar
75 ml (2½ fl oz/⅓ cup) marsala or other sweet wine

For the caramelised nuts
50 g (2 oz/¼ cup) caster (superfine) sugar
100 g (3½ oz/⅔ cup) whole blanched or unblanched almonds and pistachios

For the sauce
250 ml (8½ fl oz/1 cup) good red wine
35 g (1¼ oz/scant ¼ cup) caster (superfine) sugar
2 tablespoons runny honey
1 small strip of orange zest

First make the caramelised nuts. Line a baking tray with baking parchment. Dissolve the sugar in a small saucepan with the nuts over a medium heat. Stir with a wooden spoon and cook until the sugar starts to smell like caramel and deepens in colour. Pour on to the baking parchment and leave to set. Fill the saucepan with hot water straight away to avoid a sticky pan – be careful when doing this as it will spatter and spit. The nuts will set to a brittle toffee and should then be roughly cut with a sharp knife, or you can pop them into a food processor and give them a quick blitz. Ideally, you want them roughly chopped rather than crushed to a sandy texture.

For the *semifreddo*, line a 22 x 10 cm (8½ x 4 in) loaf tin with cling film (plastic wrap). Work quickly through the process of whipping by having everything in bowls in front of you. Beat the egg whites in a spotlessly clean bowl with an electric whisk until stiff and set aside. Use the same beaters to whisk the cream until it maintains soft peaks. Whip the remaining ingredients together until creamy and well combined, around 5 minutes.

Now, again using the beaters, briefly whisk the two creams together and then add the egg whites. Don't over-whisk but whisk just enough to combine the mixture. Pour half the mixture into the loaf tin, then add the nuts in a line down the centre so they won't be seen from the outside (reserve a few for decoration). Cover with the remaining mixture and freeze for at least 3 hours and preferably overnight. When it is frozen, remove from the tin and cover in another layer of cling film.

Make the wine sauce by reducing the ingredients in a pan to roughly a third of the original volume. It will take around 15 minutes to thicken; you can drizzle a few drops on to a cold plate to see how thick and viscous it is when cold (like making jam). When you are happy that it is thick enough, remove from the heat and allow to cool. Pour into a serving jug.

When ready to serve, peel away the cling film and place the *semifreddo* on a serving dish. Leave at room temperature for around 10 minutes before slicing and serving scattered with the reserved nuts and the wine sauce on the side.

QUINCES ALLA ANNA

Anna is a friend of ours who is widely travelled and she remembered a dish from one of her trips that tasted of perfume, fruit and spice. Together we recreated this dish with some quinces left over from making Quince Paste (see page 257). It is an easy dessert to serve with cream or ice cream and wonderful for breakfast the next day with yoghurt and toasted nuts.

Serves 4–6

2 quinces
juice of ½ lemon
2 tablespoons brandy (optional)
juice of 1 orange
100 g (3½ oz/½ cup) brown sugar
finely grated zest of ½ orange
4 cloves
1 medium cinnamon stick, broken up

Preheat the oven to 180°C (350°F/Gas 4). Core and peel the quinces and finely slice into cold water with the lemon juice – this will stop them turning black. Arrange the quince slices in an ovenproof dish so that they are slightly overlapping. Pour over the brandy (if using) and orange juice, then scatter over the brown sugar, orange zest, cloves and cinnamon. Bake for 1 hour or until lightly browned and softened inside. Halfway through the cooking time, tip the dish to one side and spoon the juices over the quinces, then continue cooking. Serve hot or allow to come to room temperature. Serve with the Rose or Saffron Ice Cream on pages 229–230.

PUMPKIN FRITTERS

These are amazing, especially with Nutella spread on top as my children do – I hate to admit it, but wow! Since all flours and pumpkins differ in moisture content it is really important to be prepared to adjust the quantity of each. Add a little more flour if necessary, until you achieve the consistency of a thick batter. You can make the batter the night before and leave it in the fridge so it's ready for a quick breakfast in the morning.

Makes approximately 20 fritters

350 g (12 oz) pumpkin, peeled, seeded
    and cut into cubes (from a 1 kg/2 lb 3 oz
    pumpkin or butternut squash)
100 g (3½ oz/¾ cup) gluten-free flour
2 eggs
2 tablespoons caster (superfine) sugar
1 heaped teaspoon baking powder
1 teaspoon ground cinnamon
pinch of salt, plus extra to serve (optional)
seed oil, for greasing
icing (confectioner's) sugar and mixed
    spice, or salt, to serve (optional)

Preheat the oven to 200°C (400°F/Gas 6). Put the pumpkin on a baking tray and cover with foil. Bake for 30–40 minutes until softened. Remove the foil and allow to cool. Put into a food processor with the remaining ingredients (except the seed oil and icing sugar mix) and blend until you have a thick batter.

Heat a large non-stick frying pan wiped with a little seed oil using a piece of kitchen paper. Dro level tablespoons of the mixture into the pan and fry for a few minutes until golden brown. The fritters will be around 7 cm (2¾ in) wide and you can cook three or four at a time. Turn them over gently when browned and fry the other side. Remove and place on kitchen paper. Scatter over the icing sugar mix for a Christmassy feel, or some salt. Eat when just cool enough to touch.

COFFEE CHOCOLATE & WALNUT CAKE

We have come across hundreds of recipes in our research that use up breadcrumbs. In fact, I might just write 1,000 recipes for breadcrumbs one day! However, I hadn't seen them used in cakes before. What a good idea! This recipe is based on one from Pina, the mother of Gregorio, the Sicilian head chef of our restaurant in Bray. It isn't suitable for hard, dry bread, more the slightly past-their-best soft white or brown interiors of a crusty loaf. To make the breadcrumbs, simply whizz in a food processor. The original recipe uses only walnuts, but we were inspired by the dark, grainy chocolate of Modica and the shot of espresso that rounds off every meal in Italy.

Serves 8–10

---

200 g (7 oz/2 cups) walnuts
50 g (2 oz/generous ¾ cup) fresh
   breadcrumbs from a wheat or
   gluten-free loaf
2 teaspoons baking powder
8 heaped teaspoons finely ground coffee
100 g (3½ oz/ scant ½ cup) chocolate or
   carob chips
100 g (3½ oz/scant ½ cup) softened
   salted butter, plus extra for greasing
125 g (4 oz/generous ½ cup) light brown
   muscovado sugar
4 eggs

Preheat the oven to 170°C (325°F/Gas 3) and generously grease a 24 cm (9½ in) (or similar size) loose-bottomed round cake tin with butter. Toast the walnuts on a baking tray in the oven for around 8 minutes or until they deepen in colour. Grind the walnuts in a food processor or chop by hand to a fine breadcrumb texture.

Mix together the walnuts, breadcrumbs, baking powder, coffee and chocolate chips in a bowl and set aside. Whisk together the butter and sugar until light and fluffy – this should take around 5 minutes. Add the eggs one by one and keep whisking. Next, use a spatula to fold the walnut mixture into the wet ingredients until combined. Pour into the cake tin and bake for 35 minutes. Test for doneness: if a skewer or toothpick inserted into the cake comes out clean, the cake is ready. Remove from the oven and leave to cool in the tin before turning out onto a plate.

RICOTTA CAKE

This triumphant cake is based on the colourful iced *cassata* cakes you see all over Sicily, only it is a much lighter version that is not difficult to make. There is an expression in Sicilian dialect, 'You are as beautiful as a *cassata*' – how romantic to be likened to a cake! If you can find potato flour, do use it as it will make the sponge lighter; if not, use cornflour. You can find potato flour in Asian shops or Italian delis. If you can get hold of sheep's ricotta all the better, for these cakes are traditionally made with ewe's milk, which has a pleasant, tangy taste.

Serves 8

For the sponge
5 eggs, separated
pinch of salt
150 g (5 oz/generous ⅔ cup) caster
    (superfine) sugar
75 g (2½ oz/½ cup) potato flour or
    cornflour
75 g (2½ oz/scant ⅔ cup) '00' flour,
    plus extra for dusting
finely grated zest of ½ lemon

For the syrup
75 ml (2½ fl oz/⅓ cup) marsala
25 ml (1 fl oz) water

For the filling
750 g (1 lb 10 oz/3 cups) ricotta
150 g (5 oz/generous ⅔ cup) caster
    (superfine) sugar
1 teaspoon finely grated orange zest
6 tablespoons marsala
25 g (1 oz/2 tablespoons) dark
    (bittersweet) chocolate (minimum
    70% cocoa solids), broken into pieces

For the coating
100 ml (3½ fl oz/scant ½ cup)
    whipping cream
250 g (9 oz/1 cup) ricotta
1 tablespoon runny honey or caster
    (superfine) sugar, to taste
200 g (7 oz) toasted flaked almonds
    or hazelnuts or pistachios
25 g (1 oz/scant ¼ cup) coarsely grated
    dark (bittersweet) chocolate
25 g (1 oz/scant ¼ cup) icing
    (confectioner's) sugar

butter, for greasing

Preheat the oven to 170°C (325°F/Gas 3) and grease and flour a 23 cm (9 in) cake tin. Whip the egg whites to soft peaks in a spotlessly clean bowl with a pinch of salt. Slowly pour in 100 g (3½ oz/scant ½ cup) of the sugar while whisking. Mix the yolks with the remaining sugar in another bowl until pale and creamy, then use a spatula to fold the two together. Sift in the two flours, add the lemon zest and fold them in. Pour into the prepared tin and cook for 30–35 minutes, until a skewer comes out clean when inserted into the centre. When cooked, remove from the tin and allow to cool on a rack. Meanwhile, make the filling by draining the ricotta and mixing the ingredients, except for the chocolate, together in a bowl.

Carefully cut a 1 cm (½ in) thick disc from the top of the cake and set aside. Next cut a 2 cm (¾ in) disc, leaving you with a final one of 1 cm (½ in). Lay one of the shallower discs back in the tin with the outside surface downwards. Next cut a circle from the thicker disc so that you are left with a ring of around 1 cm (½ in) – this will make the border around the hole for the filling. Place it into the tin and eat the centre as a cook's treat! Mix together the ingredients for the syrup and brush two-thirds over the sponge.

Fill the hole with the ricotta filling mixture. Melt the chocolate briefly in a microwave or in a bowl over a saucepan of boiling water. Spread the melted chocolate over the final disc of sponge with a palette knife. Invert this over the cake and press down lightly. Brush on the remaining syrup. Leave the cake to rest in the fridge for at least 6 hours and up to a day. Turn out of the mould.

Whip the cream to form soft peaks and fold into the ricotta and honey or sugar. Use a palette knife to spread this evenly over the cake. Finish the coating with a sprinkling of nuts, grated chocolate and icing sugar. Chill in the fridge for a minimum of 1 hour or up to a day before serving.

WATERMELON JELLIES

In the height of summer the watermelons are incredible, strongly flavoured and naturally sweet, so only make this when you have good ingredients. This is a delicate and light dessert which dates back to the time of the island's Arab conquerors. It is traditionally decorated with nuts, chopped chocolate and fragrant white jasmine flowers.

Makes 4 small tea glasses

---

30 g (1 oz/¼ cup) cornflour
500 ml (17 fl oz/2¼ cups) watermelon
  juice, passed through a sieve (about
  1 small ripe watermelon)
1 teaspoon ground cinnamon
25 g (1 oz/scant 2 tablespoons) caster
  (superfine) sugar
1–2 tablespoons rosewater, to taste
  (optional)
chopped pistachios, coarsely grated
  chocolate and jasmine flowers,
  to serve

Mix the cornflour together with a little of the watermelon juice in a bowl – if it becomes lumpy simply push it through a fine sieve with a spoon. Add this to the rest of the juice, with the cinnamon, sugar and rosewater (if using) in a saucepan and place over a gentle heat. Stir continuously and cook until thickened, then pour into glasses and chill until set. Serve with a sprinkling of pistachios, chocolate and jasmine flowers.

ALMOND & HONEY BISCUITS

These crunchy almond biscuits are from a village called Ciminna near Palermo and the recipe has been given to us by Zia Vitalba, the aunt of our friend Marco. Marco told me that foods in Sicily are either salty or sugary, as large amounts of both were used as a preservative. I have replaced the sugar in these biscuits with a small amount of honey as we found them impossibly sweet as they were.

Makes 15 biscuits

250 g (9 oz/1⅔ cups) unblanched almonds
2 egg whites
2 tablespoons runny honey
1 teaspoon ground cinnamon

Preheat the oven to 170°C (325°F/Gas 3) and line a baking tray with baking parchment. First, roughly chop the almonds to a gravelly texture using a food processor or knife. Whip the egg whites in a spotlessy clean bowl to stiff peaks with an electric whisk, adding the honey a little at a time. Fold in the almonds and cinnamon to produce a thick paste.

Use your hands to form 15 little round patties around 5 cm (2 in) wide and 1.5 cm (⅝ in) thick. Place on the prepared tray, spacing them with a gap of around 5 cm (2 in) between each one. Bake in the oven for 15 minutes or until they are set and lightly browned.

Above, clockwise from top left: Clementine & Almond Slice (see page 215); Almond & Honey Biscuits (opposite); and, Soft Almond Biscuits (see page 214).

CLEMENTINE MARMALADE

We loved this bright orange, bittersweet marmalade for breakfast on yoghurt when we were in Sicily. It is equally at home spooned over the Marsala Semifreddo on page 234, over ricotta or mascarpone, in the Clementine and Almond Slice on page 215 or just on toast. The perfume of bubbling clementines fills the house as you make it.

This will be a loose-set marmalade and fairly low in sugar compared to traditional varieties. There isn't enough sugar to enable the jars to be kept safely out of the fridge, but since we're only making a small batch it doesn't take up too much room.

**Makes approximately
1.5 kg (3 lb 5 oz)**

---

1 kg (2 lb 3 oz) clementines
juice of 2 lemons
1 litre (34 fl oz/4¼ cups) water
400 g (14 oz/2 cups) granulated sugar

Remove the stalks and hard knobbly bits at the top of the clementines and cut in half, keeping the skin on. Now roughly chop into smaller pieces by hand or in a food processor. The pieces should be no bigger than 1 cm (½ in) cubes. Put them into a large heavy-based saucepan with the lemon juice and water and bring to the boil. Turn the heat down to a simmer and allow the mixture to bubble away slowly for 1 hour. By this time the skins should have softened so that you can squash them easily with a spoon against the side of the pan and the marmalade will have thickened to a soft, runny set.

Next add the sugar and stir through. Bring to a rapid boil for around 5 minutes or until the sugar has dissolved. Pour into clean, warm jars (I do this by rinsing them out with hot water from the kettle) and screw on the lids. Allow the jars to cool and keep in the fridge for up to 1 month.

Use **3** Ways

On whipped ricotta, in the
Clementine & Almond
Slice (see page 215), in the
Sticky Finger (see
page 263)

FIG ALMOND & ORANGE CAKE WITH MARSALA

This is a nutty, dense cake packed with flavour and texture from the figs and two kinds of almonds. It works perfectly at the end of a meal with a spoonful of marscarpone and glass of dessert wine, such as the apricot-flavoured wine from Pantelleria, or with coffee in the morning, or the Vanilla Ice Cream on page 229. Figs grow wild all over the island and are dried to last through winter. Try to find dried figs that are still soft and flexible; if you can't, soak them in warm water for 30 minutes before using. Oranges of various types are available most of the year in Sicily but the most popular, the blood orange Tarocco, is only available in the winter months.

Serves 10–12

---

150 g (5 oz/scant 1 cup) whole almonds (blanched or unblanched)
250 g (9 oz/1¼ cups) soft dried figs
150 g (5 oz/scant ⅔ cup) softened salted butter
100 g (3½ oz/scant ⅔ cup) brown muscovado or caster (superfine) sugar
3 eggs, separated
200 g (7 oz/2¼ cups) ground almonds
finely grated zest of 1 small orange
1 teaspoon vanilla extract
1 teaspoon baking powder
4 tablespoons Marsala, brandy or orange juice
mascarpone, to serve (optional)

Preheat the oven to 170°C (325°F/Gas 3). Cut a circle of baking parchment measuring 34 cm (13 in) across and loosely push it into the sides a 23 cm (9 in) tart tin to line it.

Toast the whole almonds for 10–12 minutes or until the skins start to split in the oven. Remove and allow to cool. Chop by hand or put into a food processor and blitz until you have a rough, sandy texture. Set aside and then do the same with the figs.

Beat the butter and sugar together with an electric whisk until pale and fluffy. Add the egg yolks, one at a time, and beat in. Add the figs, both kinds of almonds, orange zest, vanilla extract and baking powder and fold in using a large spatula or metal spoon. Whip the egg whites to stiff peaks. Use a quarter of this to loosen the sticky almond and fig mixture by folding it in with a large metal spoon. Then gently fold in the rest of the egg whites. Pour into the prepared tin and level the top with a palette knife.

Place the tin in the middle of the oven and bake for about 35–40 minutes or until a skewer inserted into the centre of the cake comes out clean. Remove from the oven and allow to cool in the tin. When the cake is at room temperature pierce it all over with a skewer and evenly pour over the Marsala to soak it. As the edges of the baking parchment will have browned in the oven I often serve it from the lining paper on a large wooden board with a bowl of mascarpone for a rustic look.

ALMOND MILK PUDDINGS

If you are making your own Almond Milk (see page 211) for this, it is a good idea to strain it through a fine sieve before using, unless you are happy with the slightly grainy texture. I like it this way; Giancarlo likes it smooth! Homemade almond milk has a gentle flavour which is perfectly lovely as it is. If you like more punch in your desserts, think about adding a few tablespoons of amaretto or rosewater to the mixture before it sets. You will need to do this if you are using cow's milk. Do try these with shot glasses of Raspberry Granita (see page 220) and enjoy the flavours of summer and the contrasting textures.

Serves 6

40 g (1½ oz/⅓ cup) cornflour
500 ml (17 fl oz/2¼ cups) whole milk or almond milk
1 strip of lemon zest from the length of an unwaxed lemon, plus extra to decorate (optional)
40 g (1½ oz/3 tablespoons) caster (superfine) sugar
3 tablespoons amaretto liqueur or 1–2 tablespoons rosewater, to taste (optional)
3 amaretti biscuits, crushed, or 100 g (3½ oz/⅔ cup) pine nuts or edible flowers, to decorate (optional)

Mix the cornflour with a little of the milk in a small bowl. Place the lemon zest with the rest of the milk and the sugar in a saucepan to heat, just until the sugar dissolves. Add the liqueur or rosewater now, if using. Add the cornflour mixture and whisk through to avoid any lumps. When the mixture begins to thicken, pour it into heatproof glasses or moulds and let it set in the fridge for 2 hours or overnight.

Serve in the glasses for ease, or remove by running a knife around the edges of the moulds. Then dip them briefly into very hot water to loosen them. Turn out onto plates and serve, decorated if you like with pine nuts, crushed amaretti biscuits, lemon zest or edible flowers.

FARRO & RICOTTA CREAMS

This ancient recipe is still very popular, especially around the time of the festival of Santa Lucia, patroness of Syracuse, which takes place on 13 December. Wheat berries are soaked and cooked until tender and mixed with creamy ricotta. You can find precooked wheat known as *grano cotto* in Italian delis but otherwise the grain farro or, for the gluten-free, brown rice are good substitutes.

Serves 8

200 g (7 oz) wheat berries, farro
  or brown rice
600 g (1 lb 5 oz/2½ cups) ricotta
100 ml (3½ fl oz/scant ½ cup) whole milk
2 teaspoons ground cinnamon
15 g (½ oz/1 tablespoon) candied orange,
  very finely diced and a little more finely
  cut into shards
2–4 tablespoons runny honey or caster
  (superfine) sugar, to taste
4 tablespoons dark (bittersweet)
  chocolate shavings, to decorate

Soak the berries, farro or brown rice in cold water overnight. Discard the soaking water and then cook the grain of your choice in plenty of fresh boiling water until very tender and swollen. Drain and allow to cool. Meanwhile, if the ricotta is very dry, whip together with the milk to loosen it and then mix in the cooled grain, cinnamon and candied orange, and add honey or sugar to taste. Serve in bowls or glasses, decorated with a sprinkling of chocolate shavings and a few shards of candied orange.

QUINCE PASTE

If you look around antiques markets in Sicily, you will see rough moulds made from clay which were used to make *cotognata*, quince cheese or paste. They had designs and initials on them to decorate the finished cheese. Sweet quince with mature pecorino and the Almond & Pecorino Biscuits on page 258 is a lovely way to finish a meal.

Serves 12–14

---

3 large quinces
5 litres (170 fl oz/21 cups) water
800 g (1 lb 12 oz/3½ cups) caster
   (superfine) sugar

Peel, core and chop the quinces into roughly 4 cm (1½ in) cubes. Put them into a large saucepan and cover with the water. Bring to the boil, then reduce the heat. Continue to cook until the quinces become soft, around 45 minutes. To achieve a deep pink colour to the finished paste, allow the quinces to stand in the water overnight.

Drain and purée the quince flesh with a blender and then pass through a sieve. For every kilo (2 lb 3 oz) of purée you will need to add 800 g (1 lb 12 oz/3½ cups) sugar. Put the sugar and quince purée together in a large saucepan and stir frequently over a low heat until the sugar dissolves and the mixture has reduced to a thick paste. This could take up to 1 hour. If a skin forms over the surface, discard this. The mixture is ready when a spoon drawn across the top leaves a trail.

Pour the mixture into a lined small loaf tin and leave at room temperature overnight. The following day turn out of the loaf tin and eat straight away, or keep the paste in an airtight tin for up to a month.

ALMOND BISCUITS & PECORINO

This is a good time to use the almond meal left over from making Almond Milk (see page 211). However, if you do then add a little more butter to the mix as almond meal is a lot drier than shop-bought ground almonds. These biscuits are perfect with the Quince Paste (see page 257) and a pecorino cheese. They are good, too, spread with peanut butter for a healthy snack. And they travel well, so pack them up for the kids to take to school.

**Serves 8–10
(makes approximately 25 biscuits)**

200 g (7 oz/2 cups) ground almonds
50 g (2 oz) pecorino or Parmesan, grated
½ teaspoon baking powder
1 teaspoon salt
40 g (1½ oz/⅓ stick) unsalted butter,
    at room temperature
6 tablespoons water
flavouring such as fennel or sesame
    seeds, rosemary, oregano or chilli
    flakes (optional)

Preheat the oven to 170°C (325°F/Gas 3). Using your fingers mix together the almonds, cheese, baking powder, salt, butter and water to form a dough. Spread out a sheet of baking parchment and roll out the dough under another sheet of parchment to around 5 mm (¼ in). Peel off the top sheet, scatter over the flavouring of your choice, if using, and put the top sheet back in place. (I like to scatter one area with dark sesame seeds or black onion seeds, another with fennel seeds and another with pale sesame so that you can cut long biscuits that fade from one colour to another.) Roll into the dough with the rolling pin.

Slide the parchment onto a baking tray and put into the oven to bake for 15–20 minutes or until firm to the touch. Remove from the oven and cut into shapes with a sharp knife, then cool on a rack. The biscuits will keep for a couple of weeks in an airtight container.

TOASTED ALMOND

We enjoyed this ice-cold, creamy cocktail after dinner at the Grand Hotel Villa Igiea in Palermo. We were told by the cocktail maker that it was an international cocktail, but it seemed to fit Sicily so well with lovely almond flavour. Here is our version.

Makes 1

50 ml (2 fl oz) di Saronno Amaretto
50 ml (2 fl oz) Baileys or Kahlua
50 ml (2 fl oz) double cream

Fill a cocktail shaker hall full with ice. Pour the ingredients into the shaker and shake well. Strain over a few rocks into an Old Fashioned glass or tumbler and serve with an Almond & Honey Biscuit from page 246.

DUILIO

We had great fun watching the talented Alfio at the Belmond Grand Hotel Timeo prepare cocktails for us. This was one of Giancarlo's favourites as he loves Scotch.

Makes 1

25 ml (1 fl oz) Scotch whisky
15 ml (½ fl oz) Frangelico
10 ml (¼ fl oz) creme de cacao
dash Monin Caramel Syrup

Shake the ingredients over ice in a cocktail shaker. Serve in a cocktail glass.

STICKY FINGER

This refreshing cocktail (see photo opposite) is quick and easy to put together and wonderful throughout the year. Alfio from the Belmond Grand Hotel Timeo serves it with a simple mint sprig. I like to use the Clementine Marmalade from page 249, but store-bought orange marmalade is fine.

Makes 1

1 teaspoon Clementine Marmalade
  (see page 249)
15 ml (½ fl oz) fresh lemon juice
25 ml (1 fl oz) gin
50 ml (2 fl oz) Champagne

To serve
mint sprig
orange and lemon slices (optional)

Put the marmalade, lemon juice and gin into a cocktail shaker and shake to combine. Pour into a red wine glass and top with the champagne. Garnish with a mint sprig and/or orange and lemon and serve.

THE NATALIA

I love the bittersweet flavours of the Sicilian liqueur Averna. One summery evening between our restaurant manager Luca, friend Natalia and ourselves we tried various combinations of Averna with the typical citrus flavours from Sicily (all in the name of research, of course). This was the winning combination and it has become one of our favourite summer drinks.

Makes 1

25 ml (1 fl oz) Averna
25 ml (1 fl oz) Grand Marnier
15 ml (½ fl oz) lemon juice
1 length of orange peel
1 sprig of mint

Shake the ingredients together over ice in a cocktail shaker. Strain and serve in an Old Fashioned glass with a twist of orange peel, the sprig of mint and a few ice cubes.

Variation: To add a dash of sparkle, divide the Natalia between two white wine glasses and top with Prosecco or Champagne.

ACKNOWLEDGEMENTS

Thank you to ...

Marco Piraino for his incredible knowledge of Sicilian food, his impressive skills (especially at making cassata), his patience and time spent with us. You are a Sicilian star!

Karen Courtney, who accompanied me on a last-minute research visit to Palermo. I had a blast, learnt loads and completely fell for Sicily.

Sheila and Roger Brocklehurst who researched the history of Sicily (no easy task), and put together the fascinating foodie timeline.

Mimmo Zito, you are an inspiration. You made me fall for Sicily and see what true Sicilian food is about. Everyone should have the experience of eating at the fabulous Osteria Bacchus.

Paul Stratton, the Italian Specialist, for finding the best foodie places and people to visit in Sicily. Prestige Holidays for organising such great trips for us and finding brilliant places to stay.

Anne Hudson, who patiently tested recipes with me and shared her knowledge.

Steve Adams for his delicious ice-cream making skills.

Gregorio Piazza, our wonderful Sicilian Head Chef at Caldesi in Campagna.

Stefano Borella for retesting those recipes so many times.

Gino Borella for the knowledge you have passed onto us.

Caterina Valentino and her team at Hotel Palladio,

Giardini Naxos for all your help and recipes.

Ada and her team at the stunning Monaci delle Terre Nere on the slopes of Etna.

Stefano Gegnacorsi, General Manager of the incredible Belmond Grand Hotel Timeo for all your help.

Giuseppe Mazzarella and Cetti Ferrante for sharing his knowledge and research with me on Sicilian food.

Louise Ford and friends in New Jersey for their help in sourcing Sicilian recipes that travelled Brian McLeod for his Sicilian research.

Matteo Berghella and Luca Cappannari for their patient help on the cocktails.

And at Hardie Grant....

Thank you to Kate Pollard for sending us on another amazing journey, this time to discover the incredible island of Sicily. You have created another beautiful book and we will treasure it. Kajal Mistry and Hannah Roberts, thank you for bringing it all together.

Claire Warner, thank you for our stunning design. Johanna Noack, thank you for the inspired and wonderful illustrations. Helen Cathcart, we love you and your photography – we think this is the best ever!

Thank you to our literary agent Sheila Abelman for looking after us (and the citrus salad!).

Things to do in Palermo

Really interesting street food tours by Palermo Street Food
www.palermostreetfood.com

Fun and informative cooking courses and market tours by Vincenzo at Ristorante Cin Cin
www.ristorantecincin.com

Go to Ballaro and Capo markets for a fascinating, bustling view of Sicily's capital city.

See the amazing gold Palatine Chapel at the Royal Palace.

Visit a whole shop devoted to marzipan,
I Peccatucci di Mamma Andrea.
www.mammaandrea.it

Take a tour with Valentina Cusimano.
email: valecusi@msn.com
Tel: +39 3284429515

Eat at the weird and amusing Fud.
www.fud.it.

Or enjoy a bustling lunch with the locals at
Ferro di Cavallo
www.ferrodicavallopalermo.it

Or discover the tiny and lovely Osteria Dei Vespri.
www.osteriadeivespri.it

And if you are in Bagheria go to Trattoria
Don Ciccio.
www.trattoriadonciccio.it

Holidays & Hotels in Sicily we would recommend
Paul Stratton, The Italian Specialist.
www.theitalianspecialist.com

Prestige Holidays
www.prestigeholidays.co.uk

Monaci delle Terre Nere on the slopes of Etna.
www.monacidelleterrenere.it

Belmond Grand Hotel Timeo, Taormina.
www.belmond.com/grand-hotel-timeo-taormina

Hotel Principe Di Villafranca, Palermo.
www.principedivillafranca.it

Azienda Agricola Mandranova, Agrigento
www.mandranova.com

Hotel Palazzo Failla, Modica.
www.palazzofailla.it

La Dimora Hotel, Ragusa.
www.dimorapiazzacarmine.com

Algila Ortigia Charme Hotel, Ortigia.
www.algila.it

Hotel Palladio, Giardini Naxos.
www.hotelpalladiogiardini.com

Restaurants
Mimmo and Francesco Zito at Osteria Bacchus
– everyone should eat there. Find them at
Sant'Ambrogio just outside Cefalu.
*www.facebook.com/Osteria
Bacchus-800844259949950*
Tel: +39 320 144 9452

Taverna Nicastro, Modica, traditional Sicilian
food made with love.
Tel: +39 0932 945884

Sakalleo in Scoglitti for fish, and really good food.
Tel: +39 0932 871688

Apollonion in Ortigia for great fish and local
specialities.
Tel: +39 0931 483362

Enoteca Rossorubino is in Cefalu and has great
wines and antipasti. It is owned by two lovely
brothers.
Tel: +39 0921 423340

Pocho for the real couscous at S.Vito Lo Capo.
www.hotel-pocho.it

La Grotta – a wonderful restaurant owned by
father and son in a cave in Scicli.
www.lagrottascicli.it

Bibliography
Cucinare alla Siciliana by Carmelo Sammarco,
  Arnone, 1998
Flavours of Sicily, The by Anna Tasca Lanza,
  Clarkson Potter, 1996
Food of Italy, The by Claudia Roden,
  VIntage, 1998
La Cucina Siciliana by Maria Teresa di Marco
  and Marie Cecile Ferre, Guido Tommasi
  Editore, 2010
Midnight in Sicily by Peter Robb, Vintage
  Classics, 2015
Oxford Companion to Italian Food, The by
  Gillian Riley, Oxford, 2009
Sicilia by Elisia Menduni, Mondadori Electa, 2014
Sicilian Food by Mary Taylor-Simeti, Grub
  Street, 2009
Sicily by John Julius Norwich, John Murray, 2016
Sicily, Lonely Planet, 2014
Sicily, Insight Guides, 2016
Spring in Sicily by Manuela Darling-Gansser,
  Hardie Grant, 2012

ABOUT THE AUTHORS

Owners of London's Caffé Caldesi, Caldesi in Campagna in Bray, and the Marylebone La Cucina Caldesi cooking school, Katie and Giancarlo Caldesi have a passion for Italian food. They have spent over 16 years teaching students at every level, and have written nine cookbooks. Katie and Giancarlo have two children, Giorgio and Flavio.

INDEX

Sicily by Katie & Giancarlo Caldesi

First published in 2016 by Hardie Grant Books

Hardie Grant Books (UK)
52–54 Southwark Street
London SE1 1UN
hardiegrant.co.uk

Hardie Grant Books (Australia)
Ground Floor, Building 1
658 Church Street
Melbourne, VIC 3121
hardiegrant.com.au

British Library Cataloguing-in-Publication Data. A catalogue record for this book is available from the British Library.

ISBN: 978-1-78488-051-4

Publisher: Kate Pollard
Senior Editor: Kajal Mistry
Editorial Assistant: Hannah Roberts
Design: Claire Warner Studio
Illustrator: Johanna Noack
Photographer: Helen Cathcart
Food Assistant: Kathy Kordalis
Prop Stylist: Linda Berlin
Copy Editor: Lorraine Jerram
Proofreader: Laura Nickoll
Indexer: Cathy Heath
Colour Reproduction by p2d
Printed and bound in China by 1010

10 9 8 7 6 5 4 3 2 1